MOMENTS OF GRACE

Moments of Grace

Inspiring
Stories
From
Well-Known
Catholics

Al Kresta &
Nick Thomm

PUBLISHED BY ST. ANTHONY MESSENGER PRESS
CINCINNATI, OHIO

Cover and book design by Mark Sullivan
Cover image ©Tara Sgroi/Botanica/jupiterimages

LIBRARY OF CONGRESS CATALOGING-IN-PUBLICATION DATA
Kresta, Al.
Moments of grace : inspiring stories from well-known Catholics / Al Kresta and Nick Thomm.
p. cm.
Includes bibliographical references and index.
ISBN 978-0-86716-862-4 (pbk. : alk. paper) 1. Catholics—United States—Biography.
2. Catholics—United States—Interviews. I. Thomm, Nick. II. Title.
BX4670.K74 2008
282.092'273—dc22
[B]
2008034347

ISBN 978-0-86716-862-4
Copyright ©2008, Al Kresta and Nick Thomm. All rights reserved.

Published by Servant Books, an imprint of St. Anthony Messenger Press.
28 W. Liberty St.
Cincinnati, OH 45202
www.ServantBooks.org

Printed in the United States of America.

Printed on acid-free paper.

08 09 10 11 12 5 4 3 2 1

INTRODUCTION

Why You May Know More About Reality
Than Do Freud, Marx and Dawkins

O taste and see that the LORD is good!
—Psalm 34:8

I invite you to sample the following collection of spiritual stories, sometimes called "testimonies," "faith journeys" or "religious memoirs." In particular, these are stories of men and women whom I have had the pleasure and honor of knowing and interviewing. My editor, Cindy Cavnar, presented the idea for the book, based on a suggestion from John Leidy, a former designer for Servant. Nick Thomm and I discussed it. Friends were consulted.

Nick Thomm arranged the interviews that form the basis for this book. He asked people to share their most enduring spiritual experience, lesson or moment with my *Kresta in the Afternoon* radio audience. The interviews were transcribed, edited and then reviewed by the interviewees to guarantee accuracy. But this remains oral tradition. We didn't set out to create great literature but clear conversational witness to God's intervention and sometimes interference in our lives.

THE POWER AND THE LEGITIMACY OF TESTIMONY

Too often testimonies are thought to be a product of American Protestant revivalism, from Jonathan Edwards to Charles Finney to Dwight Moody to Billy Sunday to Billy Graham. Evangelical Protestantism is now and has been a powerful force in American history, a tradition to which I am very indebted.[1] But sharing the story of God's saving work in one's life did not begin in eighteenth-century evangelical Protestant America or in the German Lutheran provinces of the sixteenth century.

No, "testimony" is rooted in the experience of God's people from ancient times up to the present. Testimonies abound throughout Scripture, Christian history and general religious history. In the appendix of this book, Doctor John Love, my son-in-law, treats us to a racing, breathless overview of the use of personal testimony in the history of Catholicism.

Some look down upon this "testimony" tradition. Testimonies are unfavorably contrasted with more philosophical presentations of the Christian faith. This is a false dichotomy: Reason is not opposed to religious experience. Testimonies tell the story of God's action in history rather than present systematic descriptions of him.

Consider the phenomenon of answered prayer. Reason has little to say about particular instances of answered prayer. For example, there is no rational calculus that weighs the intensity of one's prayer relative to the depth of personal need. There is no spiritual engineering technique by which we leverage God to act. No, we learn about answered prayers largely through stories that take place away from the stage, the pulpit and the news media, stories that can be summarized in a sentence from the Psalms: "Out of my distress I called on the LORD; / the LORD answered me and set me free" (Psalm 118:5).

Dispassionate outside observers are not the best sources for this kind of evidence. We need testimony from the inside, from people who have passed through the experience and are invested in retelling it. For instance, without the testimony of survivors, we would have no real conception of the Holocaust.

Moreover, to trust testimony is normal and perfectly rational. Of course, it is only fair to expect those who share these reports to have command of their faculties and exhibit the moral qualifications that elicit trust. They must know that of which they speak. We can try to test the general reliability and integrity of witnesses, but once established, then they have to be trusted. We cannot independently verify everything they say, and that's the point of testimony: It takes us to the inside of a situation that we couldn't access apart from the witness. So there is a rational basis for confidence in religious experience and testimony.

THE EXISTENCE OF GOD

The vast majority of human beings—ancient or modern, Eastern or Western, rich or poor, educated or ignorant—have believed in a higher intelligence and power to whom their proper response is worship. This phenomenon is sometimes called the "common consent" argument for God's existence. While not logically compelling, it renders God's existence likely. It's a simple inference: If millions report that something exists, the odds are good that they are encountering something real.

We often forget how persistent and widespread is religious belief even in a so-called secular society, with no state-established church and an entertainment industry that usually portrays "good" religion as merely a private affair. (Faith is like spit. It's probably good to have some, but keep it to yourself.) Yet every American president save one has ended his inaugural address with an invocation to Providence or the almighty God, for his continued blessings on the republic.

So pervasive is religious belief among Americans that atheist philosopher Daniel Dennett laments that a secular humanist political candidate must tip the hat and utter mealymouthed appreciations for religious belief if he expects to resonate with the American people. "I don't want my candidates to lie, but I also don't want them to lose."[2] To take a seat at the victory party, the serious secular campaigner must swallow a bromide of hypocrisy.

Many of our images of religious believers and even the divine are derived from or distorted by religious television and movies like *Evan Almighty*, *It's a Wonderful Life* and *The Bells of St. Mary's* on the benign side. (On the malevolent side we've got *Cape Fear* and *Elmer Gantry*.) We see television evangelists whose clothes are as loud as their preaching and hair as well groomed as their financial appeals. George Burns and Morgan Freeman are fun-loving deities, while the Jesus of cinema often looks like a glassy-eyed flower child who just dropped mescaline and bears a slight grimace of exasperation, his feet perhaps blistered from walking the Judean countryside.

Step outside the media stereotypes, though, and look at the vast cultural, educational, historical, even theological differences between the following "believers." What unites them? Their simple affirmation of a Supreme Being:[3]

- *Plato and Bono*
- *Denzel and George Washington*
- *Johann Sebastian Bach and Alice Cooper*
- *Deepak Chopra and Vince Lombardi*
- *Dante and Babe Ruth*
- *Gandhi and Winston Churchill*

- *Christopher Columbus and Squanto*
- *Albert Schweitzer and George S. Patton*
- *Wolfgang Amadeus Mozart and Susan B. Anthony*
- *Henry Ford and Rachel Carson*
- *Ludwig van Beethoven and Duke Ellington*
- *Harriet Beecher Stowe and Robert E. Lee*
- *Rembrandt and Helen Keller*
- *Ben Franklin and Alfred Hitchcock*
- *Nelson Mandela and Douglas MacArthur*
- *Igor Stravinsky and J.K. Rowling*
- *Otto von Bismarck and Bob Hope*
- *Isaac Newton and Mel Gibson*
- *Mark Twain and Joan of Arc*
- *Francis Collins and T.S. Eliot*
- *Clara Barton and Constantine the Great*
- *Hillary Clinton and Barack Obama*
- *George W. Bush and Al Gore*
- *Abraham Lincoln and Robert Frost*
- *Oprah Winfrey and Leo Tolstoy*
- *Condoleezza Rice and Malcolm X*
- *Cesar Chavez and Roy Kroc*
- *Jimmy Carter and George Washington Carver*
- *J.R.R. Tolkien and Jackie Robinson*
- *Maria Montessori and Mickey Mantle*

Faced with a list like this (it could be multiplied indefinitely), skeptics have to wonder if maybe they're missing something. Could they be tone-deaf at life's grand symphony? Or blind at the aurora borealis? The atheist is forced to say that all of these wildly diverse human beings—creative and influential, orthodox and heterodox, pleasant and unpleasant, pious and impious—and the vast majority of human beings have been wrong about the single most important thing in life: the existence of God.

EXPERIENCE OF GOD: ANSWERS TO OBJECTIONS

There are many arguments for God's existence. Saint Thomas Aquinas, for instance, speaks of the "Five Ways." I am moved by them, but many people are not. Why not? Because the God of the Five Ways hits those people with merely the force of an inference rather than that of a personal encounter. The "theistic" arguments provide knowledge about rather than direct experience of God. And as the old Pentecostal preacher put it: "God is better felt than telt." In our own day experience tends to trump argument.[4]

On the other hand, isn't it the common complaint against religious experience that it is all so subjective? Is it "real"? Perhaps it is like the error of humorist Robert Benchley, who spent the laboratory sessions of his biology course drawing the image of his own eyelash as it fell across the microscopic field. Or like that of the Italian astronomer Schiaparelli, whose Martian "canals" may have been the veins of his own eye projected onto his telescope lens. Are spiritual experiences just a result of wish fulfillment or exotic brain chemistry?

Much has been written on these objections. Let me risk the briefest of responses.

1. We shouldn't claim that religious experience is invalid simply because it is subjective. Such an objection claims too much. After all, all experience is subjective! All claims to know are mediated through subjective selves and physical brains. As John Stuart Mill put it, "Objections which apply equally to all evidence are evidence against none."[5] Of course the experience will be subjective. The question remains, however, what is the ultimate source of the experience?

2. Further, we should remember that there is no single absolute test of truth in ordinary sense experience. Just look at a pencil placed in a glass of water. It looks bent even though it was straight when we placed it in the glass. Is it straight or is it bent?

The answer to the problem isn't less experience but more. We need more items of experience to clarify our initial perception. Lift the pencil out of the water, and run your fingers along the shaft. The pencil is straight, and now it is wet too.

The same applies to the object of religious knowledge, God. Increased familiarity with God leads to more accurate portrayals. The answer again is not to dismiss religious experience as merely subjective. The answer is to compare more experiences.

3. Along the same lines, some dismiss claims to God-knowledge by calling them names: "wish fulfillment," "projection," "disordered brain chemistry." These secular critics raise two general objections. Let's look at those.

Two General Objections

There is, first of all, the pseudo–social science objection rooted in thinkers like Feuerbach, Marx and Freud. They claim that religious experiences are the result of projection or wish fulfillment.

This has never struck me as especially convincing. How can the wish for food suggest that food is created by my hunger? Isn't my wish for food more likely to be evidence that I come from a race that normally satisfies its hunger by locating and eating food? If in fact God created us, shouldn't we expect some hunger or longing for him? After all, the Christian story begins with the claim that we were made for him.

On the other hand, maybe it's time to turn the tables. Is atheism the result of wish fulfillment? Do atheists wish God's nonexistence, since God is a potential intruder holding them morally and spiritually accountable? Do atheists reject a heavenly Father because of their pathological experience of an earthly father?[6]

Religious men and women are no more prone to gullibility than anyone else. Serious religious thinkers are part of a tradition in which certain spiritual, mental and emotional disciplines are practiced. The saints and mystics warn against self-deception. Faith is achieved often through doubt, uncertainty, sacrifice and self-critical examination. There is a premium on truth. People who take religious faith seriously in the twenty-first century are not apt to confuse wish for the real thing. They are not so easily duped.

A second objection is the pseudo–natural science objection, which reduces all human consciousness to an electrochemical show between the ears. According to this position, our experience of the divine is no more than some type of brain activity.

The problem here is the phrase "no more than." No doubt human experiences like prayer, poker and peeling potatoes all have their brain correlates. I'm sure holding a royal flush rather than a pair of deuces generates a more lively brain state, but why would this require that the brain deal us the hand? Likewise, detecting altered brain states in Carmelite nuns praying, Buddhist monks meditating or visionaries claiming to see Jesus can't settle the question of whether or not these people are encountering God. Isn't it just as likely that God equips people with the brains they need for a spiritual life?

Again, the answer isn't less experience but more. Reports of spiritual experience are numerous, broadly consistent, multicultural and transhistorical. Untold millions of men and women over several thousand years and in all cultures have reported an *experience of God*. In survey after survey since the 1960s, between 30 and 40 percent of those asked say they have, at least once or twice, felt "very close to a powerful, spiritual force that seemed to lift [them] out of [them-selves]."[7] Gallup polls in the 1990s found that 53 percent of American adults said they had had "a moment of sudden religious awakening or insight."[8]

Now, all kinds of people claim religious experience, just as all kinds of people report sense experience. Among the former, as with the latter, are a fair proportion of cranks and superstitious. But also included are a large number of keen, self-critical, straightforward, honest men and women. They possess varying degrees of spiritual maturity. Their experiences are of varying degrees of intensity and theological accuracy. But they all share some common insights into ultimate reality:

1. There is a God, and he's not me. I am not alone; there is Another.
2. We are alienated from God. Some barrier—sin, finitude, ignorance or whatever—separates us from knowledge of and perfect union with the Other.
3. We must somehow dismantle the barrier that stands between us and the Other, be reconciled with God, be conformed to his will and enter into union with him. But the means to do so lies beyond us.
4. Encountering this God confers creative moral and spiritual resources upon us. We experience a reorientation to life, personal renewal, repentance, behavioral change, love for our fellow human beings and much more.

WITNESSES

Only a relatively small number of those who have encounters with God have been able to write of them. Religious experience certainly is not limited to those few. Untold millions have prayed to, sung to, confessed to, communicated with, meditated on and preached about God variously as awesome Creator, infinite Power, cosmic Wisdom, loving Father, stern Judge, merciful Savior, sacred Wonder, infallible Guide, spiritual Companion, guiding Shepherd and intimate Friend. When these meetings with God grace the lives of gifted men and women, vivid phrases leap from their pens, trying to catch in words the momentousness of the encounter:

- Blaise Pascal's *Night of Fire*
- Augustine's *Confessions*
- Bill W.'s "flash of divine light"
- Brother Lawrence's *Practice of the Presence*
- Martin Buber's *I and Thou*
- Teresa of Avila's seventh mansion
- Moses Maimonides's "King in the Interior Rooms of the Palace"
- George Müller's "Great Provider"
- Paul of Tarsus' "Third Heaven"
- Mother Teresa's "call within a call"
- Admiral Peary's solitary encounter with "Harmony"
- John of the Cross's "spiritual marriage"
- Ignatius of Loyola's vision in the chapel of La Storta
- Francis Thompson's "Hound of Heaven"
- Faustina Kowalska's Christ of the Divine Mercy
- Immanuel Kant's "starry heavens above...and...moral law within"
- Thérèse of Lisieux's "first kiss of Jesus" in the Eucharist

And what of the uncountable men and women with diverse and sundry dreams, visions, revelations, healings and answered prayers?

Or all those who rely on the "Greater Power" of the Twelve Steps?

Or those millions who have met the Father of Mercies while hearing the words of absolution in the sacrament of penance?

It's possible that all such reports are delusional, but we should then ask ourselves how reliable or sane or intelligent are the people who report these delusions as peak, transformative experiences and who then go on to live lives of service, art or genius. As Charles Raven put it: "If these be mad then madness is more beautiful, more reasonable, more beneficent, more effective than sanity."[9]

Can you read the Beatitudes and imagine that Jesus of Nazareth was emotionally unstable? Was Moses not in touch with some great organizing principle or Person? If you think not, which is the first of the Ten Commandments you want your neighbor to break?

CONDITIONS OF KNOWING

The question must be asked: "Why, if God is really there, if he is objectively real, are some people unaware of him?" Can't everyone who looks see Mount Rushmore?

Yes, if they meet the conditions for seeing it. They must be "qualified observers." They must travel to the location or see a photograph, a painting or video show. They must have sufficient light and healthy optic nerves and not be in a coma.

In fact, not everyone can see Mount Rushmore. Some people are literally blind, unsighted; they aren't qualified observers. Few people are qualified to know the monument as an object to be climbed, for scaling it requires a different set of conditions and skills: physical stamina, climbing know-how and the desire and the time to accomplish such a feat.

All knowing involves meeting certain conditions, and these conditions change depending on what or whom we are trying to know. The conditions required to know a piece of limestone require nothing more than that I pick it up, break it and chalk with it. To know a rosebush requires that I provide proper conditions for its growth and allow time for its buds to open. When it comes to sentient creatures that can move about, knowledge gets trickier. I must meet the condition of not scaring them off. Perhaps to know them I will need to feed, pet or train them.

But when it comes to knowing other human beings, we must be prepared for trouble. The other person might say, "No, I will not let you know me." In this case the initiative between the knower and the known is roughly fifty-fifty. Of course, when it comes to God, the initiative is almost entirely on the part of God. He must reveal himself.

What are the conditions that put us in the best position to expect a visitation from God? The Quaker philosopher D. Elton Trueblood proposes a list as good as any I've seen:

1. *A natural reverence.* One might suppose this to be the result rather than the precondition of an encounter with God. But this reverence is simply openness to the possibility, the opposite attitude of the scorner, the braggart, the profane and the supercilious.

2. *The child spirit.* This is the sense that we are children playing on the shore of an uncharted ocean with unashamed expectancy of what there is to learn (see Matthew 11:25; 18:3–4; Mark 9:37; Luke 10:21).[10]

3. *Quietness.* "Be still and know that I am God" (Psalm 46:10). Lay aside the preoccupation with busyness and the pressure of circumstance.

4. *Moral obedience.* The person who strives to do the right thing knows that he often fails. But the very effort clears the spiritual senses. "For he who does not love his brother whom he has seen, cannot love God whom he has not seen" (1 John 4:20; see John 7:17).

5. *A paradoxical combination of aloneness and togetherness.* Jesus taught, "When you pray, go into your room and shut the door and pray to your Father who is in secret" (Matthew 6:6). On several occasions he went apart from the crowd and even from his disci-

ples to pray (see Mark 1:35). But just as well, all who seek to know God must find their place in worship, the love of others and the fight to eliminate evils that burden those they love. There is an incoming and outgoing tide of fellowship and solitariness.[11]

These conditions don't close the door to anybody. But they do help us understand who is a "qualified observer" of things spiritual. Just as we expect those who share their knowledge of the Milky Way to have learned to use a telescope, so we expect those who share their first-hand encounters with God to have some "training," which is available to all even if not availed of. The initiative remains with God, but the presence of these preconditions seems to render a person more apt to hear from God.

AUTHENTIC ACCOUNTS

Even some Christians, however, are suspicious of reports of religious experience. The Catholic Church herself has always warned against misguided enthusiasm. Furthermore, an individualistic emphasis on "my" story sometimes works against the Church as the corporate personality, the body of Christ.[12]

However, Saint Thomas wasn't in doubt about the experiences of the saints. Nor is the Church ashamed of its mystical doctors, like Teresa of Avila and John of the Cross. Nor does the Church ignore claims of private revelations, some of which she approves, as at Fatima.

The Church also requires each diocese to maintain an exorcist; this conviction that there is current diabolical experience is backhanded recognition that there is current divine experience. The Church continues to investigate alleged healings offered as evidence in the causes of potential canonized saints. And of course the Church believes that at each Mass Christ, acting through the priest, reveals himself in the breaking of the bread (see Luke 24:35).

Cardinal Joseph Ratzinger (now Pope Benedict XVI) taught us how to engage widespread agnosticism. The question of God, he says, involves the totality of our lives. We must use all the faculties of perception we have been given. These include "listening to the message that is brought to us by our own existence and by the world in general; a vigilant attentiveness vis-à-vis the discoveries and the religious experience of humanity; and the decisive and persevering employment of our time and our internal energy on this problem, which concerns each one of us personally."[13]

This book tries to listen "to the message brought to us by our own existence" and sensitize us to the religious discoveries of our fellows. That is why the unwritten first sentence of each of the following accounts is simply *Tell me a story of you and your God.*

Al Kresta
June 29, 2008
Solemnity of Saints Peter and Paul

ONE

Damascus Road

•

•

•

•

•

•

NORMA McCORVEY
Roe No More

Human life must be respected and protected absolutely from the moment of conception. From the first moment of his existence, a human being must be recognized as having the rights of a person—among which is the inviolable right of every innocent being to life.

—*CCC*, 2270; see Congregation for the Doctrine of the Faith,
Donum vitae, I, 1

Norma McCorvey is best known as Jane Roe from the 1973 decision legalizing abortion, *Roe* v. *Wade*. Ironically, McCorvey, who was twenty-one years old when the case was filed, never did have an abortion.

After her dramatic conversion to Christ in 1995, Norma began a pro-life ministry now called Roe No More Ministry.[1] She coauthored *Won By Love: Norma McCorvey, Jane Roe of Roe v. Wade, Speaks Out for the Unborn as She Shares Her New Conviction for Life* and later updated it with a supplement, "My Journey Into the Catholic Church." For in August 1998, she was received into full communion with the Catholic Church by Father Frank Pavone and Father Edward Robinson,[2] under the sponsorship of Detroit-area pro-life activist Lynn Mills, who first introduced me to Norma and her rollicking story.

Norma: I was raised in a Jehovah's Witness–Roman Catholic family.[3]

Al: So from the beginning there was religious conflict in your life?

Norma: Yes. And I got involved with the hippie movement and drugs. I was at the forefront of the abortion movement before it was even an issue. Then I was a wild child out in California, with the movement to bring the troops home, just being downright ornery. I have to kind of laugh, because through all this the Lord opened up a whole new world to me.

Al: Did you even imagine such a world existed?

Norma: Not in my foggiest or wildest of dreams. I never thought for one instant that I would belong to any kind of church, especially the Catholic Church.

Al: How did you find Christianity even a plausible life option? At the time of your conversion to Christ, as I remember it, you were working in an abortionist's office.

Norma: I worked in abortion clinics from 1991 to 1995. One day I started paying more attention to how the abortionist treated women. I called him on it; he told me to take a Valium and not to worry about it. I said, "I don't have any Valium, and I want to talk about it now!"

One lady who came into the first abortion clinic I worked in said she was pregnant with a little girl. The woman said she had had some sort of test done before she came in. Well, she wanted a little boy. She told me, "If you can't have what you want, then why have anything at all?"

I thought, "You are just too weird for me," and I'm strange, you know? The abortionist got wind of my attitude and sent me home.

I stopped at a drive-through beer barn and got a case of Corona. When I got home I pulled the biggest yahoo drunk of my entire life. I started ripping pro-abortion stuff off my apartment walls—

newspaper clippings, T-shirts, buttons, banners, posters—and I made a fire right there. I burnt all that stuff to a crisp.

When the firemen came up to the apartment, I said, "I'm drunk as Ol' Cooter Brown, and I'm burning all this junk."

They asked, "Well, why are you burning it now, in the middle of July?"

I said, "When you have an awakening, you just do it."

The abortionist called and asked if I had "corrected my attitude." I don't think I have to tell you, Al, what I told him.

Al: But then you went to another abortion clinic to work.

Norma: It never got any better. One was filthy. At another, where I was a telephone counselor, the supervisor came into the little room where we worked and told me that I had a 98 percent show rate. I said, "What do you mean?" She said, "You get three dollars for every first-trimester abortion you schedule and five dollars for every second-trimester abortion." I sat there for a few minutes, and I thought, "What in the world is she talking about?" I didn't know beans about the abortion industry.

One day a bunch of Christians from Operation Rescue were out in front of the abortion mill praying over my truck, and I couldn't have that. So I went outside. That's when I met Father Robinson. I looked at him and said, "Father, are you lost?"

He said, "No, no, I'm supposed to be here, I'm praying like the others."

I said, "Father, I didn't know priests came out into the streets and prayed."

He asked, "Do you work here?"

I said yes, and he asked, "Why do you do that?" I said, "I never really asked myself that."

This was the saintly priest who later gave me my *Catechism* and my first Bread of Life, and he has been my spiritual guide every since. Gosh, I'm almost crying. Father Robinson is ninety-three years old, and he still helps with the ministry.

Al: When did Flip Benham, leader of Operation Rescue, enter the picture? I know he played a role in your conversion to Christ.[4]

Norma: He was very instrumental in my conversion. Mr. Flip shared his testimony with me and told me what a big ol' sinner he had been down in Kissimmee, Florida, where he operated a saloon. I didn't understand why he was telling me this. But when he finished his story, he said, "And that's my testimony."

I thought, testimony? I'd heard of doing testimony in a courtroom, but I'd never heard of testimony from Christians. It just kind of tickled me.

Flip told me to go home and look up Deuteronomy 30:19. ("I call heaven and earth to witness against you this day, that I have set before you life and death, blessing and curse.") He didn't know that I was such a heathen that I had to go across the street and borrow a Bible.

A couple days later I saw Mr. Flip again, and I said, "Well, I read that verse you gave me the other day, but I don't understand it."

He said, "Do you like doing what you're doing?"

I said, "No, not particularly, but what can I do?"

He said, "Well, you know you can come over to our side."

And I said, "Yeah, right."

Al: So when did you say, "I'm going to cross the line here; I'm going to choose life"?

Norma: It was one Saturday night. Little Emily Mackey was then seven years old.[5] She had been coming around the abortion clinic with her mother, who was part of Operation Rescue. For months she had been after me to come to church with her and her family. Finally I said yes, not because I suddenly felt a great need in my life for God but because I was tired of telling Emily no. Her mother was skeptical.

Al: Where did they take you?

Norma: We went to Hillcrest Church.[6] Pastor Morris Sheats's sermon that night was on John 3:16. He read it out loud: "For God so loved the world that he gave his only-begotten Son, that whoever believes in him should not perish but have eternal life." Then he asked if there was anyone who wanted to come and meet Jesus.

I didn't know that Jesus would just come to this church. But see, I didn't understand what he meant. So I held up my hand. Then he said, "OK now, I know where you're sitting," and I thought, "Oh, shoot, busted again."

He went on: "I would like you to come down to the prayer rail."

I didn't hear the first part, just the rail part, and I thought, "Oh, my, they are going to put me on one of those rails and stretch my body; they are going to torment me."

But I got up; I was a brave little person. I went down to the prayer rail, and the pastor looked at me and said, "Kneel," and I said, "OK."

But I thought, "They are going to behead me." When you are a heathen and you don't understand the way churches work, you think of all these horrible things, like, "They will probably bathe in my blood."

Al: To the contrary, *you* were washed in the blood of the Lamb. So there you were at the prayer rail, and you responded to God's love in Christ. What then drew you to the Catholic Church?

Norma: To put it simply, Al, I saw all the Catholics coming out to the abortion mill, once I was with Operation Rescue, and they were so reverent. They just glowed. It really won my heart.

One night on the way to an Operation Rescue rally, I asked that "radical" Father Pavone, "Father Frank, is there such a thing as a born-again Catholic?"[7]

He said, "Absolutely, Miss Norma. Are you thinking about joining the Catholic Church?" and I said, "Yeah, Father, I think I am."

So he gave me my first rosary and my first book on how to say my prayers. I was truly blessed. Eventually I just decided, "I want to join the Catholic Church. I want to join the largest and the biggest and the best church in the whole world." Now I'm hard-core Catholic, and I make no apologies for it.

Of course, my message when I go out to speak is strictly ecumenical. In Roe No More Ministry, we turn away no one who is seeking help. There isn't a "Baptist God" or a "Methodist God" or a "Catholic God." There is one God, and everyone is equal in his sight.

In 1995 there were eleven abortion clinics in Dallas; today there are only four. Praise God! All of the ones in which I worked are closed.

In the Company of the Great King and All His Family

> *All men are called to belong to the new People of God. This*
> *People, therefore, while remaining one and only one, is to be*
> *spread throughout the whole world and to all ages in order*
> *that the design of God's will may be fulfilled.*
>   —*CCC*, 831, quoting *Lumen Gentium*, 13, §§ 1–2; see John 11:52

I first met Steve and Janet Ray when I was in knickers and sporting an Amish beard and a white wig. I was playing the role of the evangelical apologist Francis Schaeffer on a panel of theologians, philosophers and scientists in a six-way scripted argument called "The Genesis Wars." Steve, with characteristic boldness, sought me out afterward and told me that he had just returned from Schaeffer's rescue mission for intellectuals, *L'Abri*, in Huémoz, Switzerland. Our families have been fast friends ever since, now over twenty-five years.

It's truly amazing to see how the love of God's Word, planted in Steve's early years, has mushroomed into a dynamic Bible teaching ministry. Steve is a Catholic convert, author, teacher, conference speaker and video producer. He has produced, directed and hosted the award-winning landmark film series *The Footprints of God: The Story of Salvation From Abraham to Augustine* and is the author of *Crossing the Tiber: Evangelical Protestants Discover the Historical*

Church and *Upon This Rock: St. Peter and the Primacy of Rome in the Scriptures and the Early Church,* as well as *St. John's Gospel: A Bible Study Guide and Commentary for Individuals and Groups.*

Steve and Janet are certified guides to the Holy Land. For information about their pilgrimages, see www.catholicconvert.com.

Steve: When I was four years old, I knelt in front of the green vinyl couch in our living room while my mother coached me to ask Jesus into my heart. That's when it all began for me. But the two-part experience I want to talk about comes from later periods of my life. Let me tell it as an extended analogy.

First of all, imagine meeting a king, entering his court and spending time with him. He enjoys you and teaches you. But secondly, later in life, he trusts, loves and respects you enough to introduce you to his whole family. My story covers these two aspects of my spiritual life.

I met Jesus for myself when I was about thirteen or fourteen years old. We met in an evangelical Protestant setting, because the Rays were Baptists. We tried to read and follow the Bible in the old evangelical or even fundamentalist Baptist tradition.

Mom kept Christian radio on as often as possible, hoping that subliminally the gospel would get into her kids' heads. After all, the Bible says, "Train up a child in the way he should go, / and when he is old he will not depart from it" (Proverbs 22:6).

One night I heard a Billy Graham sermon on TV. I don't remember any details from it. But I remember having a palpable experience of Jesus Christ. Instead of going forward in a church for an altar call, I walked down our very long driveway. We lived in the country, so the night was very dark. I looked up at the stars, realizing I was small and vulnerable. I was stirred by Graham's message (whatever it was), and

I was feeling the hymn that at the crusade's end invited me to come to Jesus, "just as I am, without one plea, but that thy blood was shed for me."[1]

That night I gave my life to Jesus, telling him, "I'm gonna give my life to you, and no matter what it takes, I'm gonna serve you and love you and obey you."

A great peace swept over me, and I knew he was really there, that he had created the cosmos and me as a part of it. That I was in his hands I couldn't deny. Nor could I deny that my sins were forgiven. I also knew that somehow as I grew older, I would love and serve him with my whole life.

Al: You weren't handed a blueprint of your future life, but you had that confidence.

Steve: Right. It would be like meeting the king and hearing him say, "Young man, I like you, and I'm going to do something with you. I will accept you as my subject." This King's realm was big and majestic, and I was very pleased that he had recognized me and promised that I could be a part of his kingdom and be useful in his service.

Then fast-forward to seventeen years old. I'd gone through some stubborn, rebellious years. I didn't want to go to church. Like many kids, I didn't want to be with my parents. (I think that's built in by God to help you break away and become your own person.) Yet I remembered the invitation that the Lord had given me.

I met a basketball player, a black belt in karate, who wasn't much older than I. He really knew Jesus personally. What had happened to me when I was thirteen now reawoke in me. I had what we'd call not a born-again experience but a rededication of my life to Christ.

My house was full of Bibles, because my mom left them around hoping we'd pick one up and read it. So I began to read the Bible. All of a sudden I had a thirst for the Word of God, to understand more about Jesus, to live as a Christian and to tell other people.

The twist was that I didn't want my mom and dad to know that I was becoming what they were. I hid my Bible between the mattresses of my bed. (I know kids hide different kinds of things between the mattresses, but I hid my Bible there.) At night after everybody was asleep, I'd lock my door, read the Bible, pray and ask Jesus to help me be a good Christian.

I had a favorite tree in the woods, under which I would sit for an hour every afternoon after school. (I used a stopwatch.) With the Bible and a prayer list in front of me, I learned to pray. I was getting a feel for this King and what it was like to be in his courtroom: to plead for other people, to see that he would look on me with favor and to study the original documents of his kingdom.

Now I need to fast-forward again to a time in my life when you, Al, actually played a significant role. I'll get choked up talking about it if I'm not careful.

Al: I might mist up along with you.

Steve: This happens a lot when I try to tell this story. This is when the King—who'd invited me into his private realm, to know him and communicate with him—loved me enough to say, "I'm going to introduce you to my family." This is when I came to find the Catholic Church.

It was no longer just me and the King, me and Jesus and the Bible. I now realized that the King had a much larger kingdom, composed of a lot of other people of different colors and races, and he loved all of them as much as he loved me. Now I get to know them under his hierarchy, his leadership, his rule and tradition. He had more to share with me than just his book. (Paradoxically, the Bible has become dearer to me than when it stood alone without the teaching authority of the Church.)

It was as if I walked out of his small courtroom and into the fullness of his kingdom, into a great hall that was filled with all his people with their great feasts. He brought me out one day and said, "Everybody, I'd like you to meet Steve Ray." That's very much what it was like for me and my wife, Janet, to come into the Catholic Church.

And you were the one, Al, who opened the door, invited us in and made it possible for us to consider this. We began to read and study because I wanted to disprove you after you'd become a Catholic. But also so I could immunize myself from actually becoming a Catholic.

Al: The details of those conversations are still with me.

Steve: And with me too. I began to read many of the King's documents and those of the early Christians. Somehow I had always assumed that the early Church was Protestant in its beliefs and practices—*like me*. I imagined that the early Church was a simple, primitive assembly of believers without the accretions of the papacy and the veneration of Mary and statues. Somewhere along the road, I assumed, Catholicism got mixed up in there, and the train fell off the tracks and rolled down the hill.

But when I began to read those first loyal subjects of the King—those who had written about the King very early on, those who even knew his first followers, the apostles—I realized that it wasn't the early Church that had gone off the tracks and rolled down the hill: It was me. I found out that my "tradition" had started fifteen hundred years later at the so-called Protestant Reformation.

So as I began to learn more, I embraced the King's kingdom and not just the King, whom I had always loved. I embraced the ministers of the King, his clergy, those who rule the kingdom with him. There was one in particular named Peter, who carries the keys of the kingdom around with him in the name of Benedict XVI today. Yes, he still carries those keys after two thousand years.

Nothing in my life has affected me and my family so profoundly. I am so grateful to God for introducing himself to me when I was thirteen and for introducing me to his family when I was thirty-nine.

Al: For all the years we've been friends, you have been a committed Christian, but when the King drew you closer and introduced you to the members of his kingdom, you became about as fruitful a disciple as I have ever known through your teaching, preaching, writing and filming.

Steve: Well, thank you for those kind words, but the King gave me everything.

Monica Migliorino Miller
That Hidden Face

*[A]ll the faithful, whatever their condition or state—though
each in his own way—are called by the Lord to that perfection
of sanctity by which the Father himself is perfect.*
—*CCC,* 825, quoting *Lumen Gentium,* 11, §3

Monica Migliorino Miller is a professor of sacred
theology at St. Mary's College of Madonna University in Orchard
Lake, Michigan. She is the author of *Sexuality and Authority in the
Catholic Church* and *The Theology of* The Passion of the Christ,
which is the definitive treatment of the theological and biblical material used by Mel Gibson in his production of *The Passion of the Christ.*
Doctor Miller is also director of Citizens for a Pro-life Society and a
vigorous on-air guest. She and her husband, Edmund, have, by example and exhortation, modeled street-level Catholic activism to many,
including two of my sons who were privileged to be Edmund's students at Spiritus Sanctus Academy in Ann Arbor, Michigan.

Monica: Most people don't know that I have a degree in theater. "My
quest" as a teenager and young adult was to become a famous movie
actress. Somehow this would confer upon me a kind of greatness, an
earthly immortality, so that when I died my persona, my image,
would live on.

I was consumed by this quest. I ate and drank and slept it. I was driven to rise above and conquer the world. When I was eighteen or nineteen years old, I wrote a poem that contained the line, "My soul longs for glory. To die and to get it from God is a hollow victory."

Al: That is an ambitious line for a teenager. It sounds like the ancient Greek pagan ideals of glory, honor, fame.

Monica: Yes, I had to achieve it myself. It was the very pagan idea of rising above the rest in conquering the world.

Consumed as I was by this desire for fame and fortune and so on, if I tried out for a part in a play and did not get it, I was crushed. My self-esteem and sense of identity were bound up in this kind of success.

Al: You were in the "performance trap" in the most literal way.

Monica: That's exactly right.

I went to Southern Illinois University to study theater when I was about nineteen years old. This university is known for one of the best theater programs in the Midwest. Believe me, it is also one of the most secular places on earth. But here is the funny thing: *God entered into this most decadent environment.*

It was there that I landed a part in Tennessee Williams's *Suddenly Last Summer.*[1] I was to play a nun, Sister Felicity. Since I had a Catholic upbringing, God did have something to work with.

My role required me to dress in a habit. With that simple costume change, a whole part of reality was opened to me—religious life, convent life. I started to read about convents and nuns.

I suppose if I went back to the stacks of the library at Southern Illinois University today, I would probably say that it was a bad collection. But at the time I didn't know anything, and I thought it was a great collection. As soon as I finished one book, I would turn it in and run back to the stacks and find another book. I read and read and read, until finally I landed on "the right one." You know how you go to the shelf, and a book sort of falls into your hands?

Al: Yes. The Divine Librarian had this one on hold for you. What was it?

Monica: It was a biography, one of the really great biographies of Saint Thérèse of Lisieux, the Little Flower. It's called *The Hidden Face*.[2] If I had to say there was a book that really changed me, it was this book.

I opened the front cover, and a photograph of a nun stared me in the face. It was Saint Thérèse of Lisieux about three months before she died. Her girlish look had been replaced by a more profound, mature, even sad one. And I resolved that whatever she had been, whatever convent she had belonged to, I was going there! And I had never even heard of Saint Thérèse of Lisieux.

Al: It sounds as if you were doing more than entering into a role. Were you aware that what was going on inside you was more than character preparation?

Monica: Absolutely. I returned to Mass and confession. For the first time in my life I really believed. I started to take my faith as an adult seriously.

What's so ironic is that I had been consumed with this quest to become the great and famous actress, but the part I ended up getting led me to a complete 180-degree turn. So now this aspiring actress was ready to enter a cloister. The play was in May 1974. By September I had changed my whole idea of what I was going to do with my life.

Al: There is also great irony in the title of the book, *The Hidden Face*, because you certainly had no intention of hiding yours.

Monica: That's exactly the opposite of what I was going to do with myself. But now I wanted to become anonymous to the world. No one would ever know who I was except for the sisters and my family.

This period in my life was filled with tremendous personal and interior turmoil. I had no spiritual direction and did not know how to get it.

Al: But you did have a new ideal.

Monica: Yes, I wanted to be a saint. I wanted to be whatever Saint Thérèse of Lisieux was. I had to be a Carmelite nun. I had to be enclosed. I had to give absolutely everything to God, with no reserve. I shifted all of my energy into this quest to be holy, but to be holy according to my own idea. Let me explain.

Al: Please.

Monica: I quit school and went back home and lived with my parents and siblings. They thought I was absolutely nuts. I kept telling them to take their faith seriously. Stop swearing. Stop being lazy. Start going to Mass. Become a saint. I was trying to evangelize my folks, and they were going out of their minds with my freshly minted religious conversion. We didn't know how to talk with one another.

I had no friends. I was completely on my own trying to figure things out. I found a Carmelite monastery in Des Plaines, Illinois.[3] For about two years I tried to find a vocation to that monastery. But I never had an instant of peace. Constant anxiety filled my heart.

Finally I realized I didn't have a vocation—at least not yet. But what had happened to me was still very, very important. So I decided to go back to Southern Illinois and finish my degree. Maybe after that I'd go back and try to get into Carmel.

I started to learn to pray and had some great instructors: Saint John of the Cross and Saint Teresa of Avila. Southern Illinois has a gorgeous campus, with a lake called Thompson Lake. I would ride my bike out there, with a doughnut and coffee. I would perch myself at the end of the pier and "commune with nature." After I ate my donut and drank my coffee, I would say a rosary.

One particular day as I was praying the rosary, I came to "Thy kingdom come, Thy will be done," and it was as though I was saying those words for the first time. I almost choked on them. "Thy will be done."

This was an illumination to me. In order to find the will of God, I had to give up mine. But to do that was to give up an ideal, a picture in my head and an idea in my heart about what it meant to be great, even what it meant to be holy. It was like throwing myself off a cliff: Would God be there to catch me?

I decided to give up what I thought I should do in pursuing this Carmelite vocation and empty myself. I don't think I'm saying too much when I say that this is the foundation of Christian spirituality: Give up your will, and let God's will be done in you. This is personalizing the experience of Jesus in the Garden of Gethsemane: "Not my will, but yours, be done" (Luke 22:42; see Matthew 26:36–46; Mark 14:32–43).

Al: So God led you down a path that was different from either of those you had envisioned for yourself.

Monica: Exactly. And I can see now that he put me in the place where I can best serve him. Isn't he amazing?

Ralph Martin

No Retreat From the Truth

> *In Jesus Christ, the whole of God's truth has been made man-*
> *ifest. "Full of grace and truth," he came as the "light of the*
> *world," he is the Truth.*
>
> —*CCC*, 2466, quoting John 1:14; 8:12; see also 14:6

Ralph Martin has been a leader in renewal movements in the Catholic Church for many years. He is the president of Renewal Ministries (www.renewalministries.net) and sponsor of the weekly television program *The Choices We Face*. He is the author of many books, including *Hungry for God: Practical Help in Personal Prayer, The Catholic Church at the End of an Age: What Is the Spirit Saying?* and *The Fulfillment of All Desire: A Guidebook for the Journey to God Based on the Wisdom of the Saints.*

Ralph also serves as director of graduate theology programs in the New Evangelization at Sacred Heart Major Seminary in Detroit.

Ralph: I grew up in a good Catholic family. I believed in the Lord, loved him and really wanted to know his will and do it.

Then along came the world, the flesh and the devil,[1] and I became attracted to the world, not even the sinful world but just the world. I wanted to break out of my Catholic ghetto and discover "reality." I awakened to literature and declared philosophy as my major.

Al: You were at the University of Notre Dame, America's most prestigious Catholic university, hungry for truth, and yet conviction of truth was eluding you.

Ralph: The problem was probably me. The answers were there, but I wasn't eager to acknowledge a spiritual and moral authority in my life. It was the 1960s—existentialism,[2] brave protests, noble rebellion and all those things. Even though I wouldn't have said that there was anything wrong in my life, it was kind of disintegrating.

Al: Were you continuing to worship?

Ralph: I had stopped going to Mass and was intellectually rebellious and morally confused. I was out on the street picketing against the establishment. The literary, intellectual people who were "really smart" rejected everything Catholic and gave me books from the "forward" European thinkers. It was a crazy environment, which I didn't know at the time was crazy.

Al: Yes. I'm one of many with scars to show. What turned you around?

Ralph: A friend invited me to make a Cursillo retreat.[3] I said yes, even though I looked down on those kinds of things.

Al: Why did you look down on them?

Ralph: I joked with my friend that people were going to sing songs, hold hands, draw pictures, have a warm experience and call it "God." I wasn't going to compromise my intellectual integrity with crazy, subjective stuff like that. (I thought I had intellectual integrity at the time.)

But anyway, here I was going to Cursillo, and all I can say is that I felt impressed just by the presentation of the plan of God. You know, a loving God created the universe, human beings fell and Christ came to redeem us. I hadn't heard a really clear, coherent presentation of the Christian faith for a long, long time.

Al: It hung together. There was a simple beauty to it that went beyond the rational.

Ralph: Absolutely. There was a depth to it. I thought, "Gee, whoever invented this was pretty smart." Plato and Nietzsche I admired as influential philosophers, but during the retreat I began to get the feeling that maybe this Cursillo presentation was coming from the mind of God.

Then they began to talk about Jesus, and I felt a little uncomfortable. It sounded a little too up close and personal. Couldn't we just talk about the Second Person of the Trinity? Maybe his mom could call him Jesus, but it seemed awfully forward for me to be on a first-name basis with the deity.

There was something going on in these people's lives that wasn't going on in my life. Either they were deluded, or there was something real there. Then they began to talk about sin, and I thought they were just describing normal college life.

Al: I suspect that what you facetiously refer to as "normal college life" was intense, expensive and destructive to the soul.

Ralph: I really struggled with that. But on the last day of the Cursillo, I felt the Lord's mercy fall on me. I went to confession, repented and was reconciled with the Lord and the Church. Toward the end of the day, God's love came into my heart, and I was graced with a tremendous experience of Jesus. It wasn't that I saw him with my eyes, but I "saw" him.

Al: Could it be chalked up to emotion?

Ralph: No, it wasn't an emotional experience; rather I experienced him, in that mysterious way in which the living Lord communicates himself to someone.

Al: It was a personal acquaintance. You experienced the presence of Another.

Ralph: Yes. He was there, he was real, and that meant that this Christian thing was true. He really was the Son of God. He really had died for our sins. He really was risen for us, and he was alive and here, now.

I had this tremendous experience of love for the Lord and his loving me. I just felt like, "*Wow!* I don't know what else is going to happen in my life, but I have just discovered the place at the center, the truth." I had found the truth, and he is Jesus Christ.

Al: This is a very powerful experience. How long did you live in the afterglow of it? How long did it last?

Ralph: Well, it's lasted more than forty years! And I'm hoping it's going to last until the day I die.

Al: [Laughing] Likewise.

Ralph: I also experienced a tremendous desire to tell other people: "Do you know that Christianity is true? Do you know that Jesus Christ really is the Lord? Do you know that he is here? Do you know that sin messes up our lives?" So at the same time I discovered the Lord and was reconciled with the Church, I also received this call to evangelization.

Al: You met the Messenger, embraced his message, and he commissioned you for his mission. Did you have any big letdown afterward?

Ralph: I had the usual trials and tribulations, and it took me a while to get everything all sorted out and to figure out the implications of Jesus being Lord.

Al: But you had a good basic launch.

Ralph: Absolutely. This is what drives my life. My initial rediscovery of the truth that Jesus is Lord continues to move me. God continues to have mercy on me, and he gives me the grace to keep on believing, keep on loving, keep on hoping and keep on telling others about him.

Al: How important was the setting of your conversion, the fact that you were part of a structured retreat?

Ralph: Many people have come to a renewed knowledge of the Lord through structured retreats. Saint Ignatius said that if he could just get somebody to do the Spiritual Exercises, there was a good chance that that person would discover the Lord.[4]

It is good to set oneself apart for a while. You're away, not doing your e-mail and keeping up with daily business. On retreat you are able to pay attention to the interior movement of God. You are able to disconnect from what our friend Teresa Tomeo calls "noise."[5] On retreat you are able to "be still, and know that I am God" (Psalm 46:10). You are able to pay more attention to God. If the people running the retreat are speaking God's word, there is a good chance that something will connect.

Further, with Cursillo the leadership enlists people to pray for those who are making retreats. They fast and offer sacrifices. It was deeply moving to me that people I didn't know wanted me to discover the Lord, and they were willing to pay a price for it.

Al: That weekend changed your whole life and, through your apostolic work, the lives of thousands. Without that retreat and encounter with God, do you think you would have fallen into despair?

Ralph: I don't think I'd be alive today if I hadn't gone on that Cursillo. My life was falling apart. The spirit of academia seemed to point to nothing: no answers, no truth, no hope, no solution to suffering and death. I think that would have driven me to profound despair and desolation.

When I think of that, I just have to thank God for his abounding mercy toward me.

TWO

Asleep in the Light

•

•

•

•

•

•

PATRICK MADRID
Not Surprised By Truth

> *The Catholic Church has always offered and still offers to the sacrament of the Eucharist the cult of adoration, not only during Mass, but also outside of it ... [for] the solemn veneration of the faithful.*
> —*CCC*, 1378, quoting Pope Paul VI, *Mysterium Fidei*, 56

Patrick Madrid is one of America's most productive and respected Catholic apologists. He's conducted hundreds of seminars and conferences, in English and Spanish, at parishes and universities across the United States and around the world. He is the publisher of *Envoy* magazine, an award-winning journal of Catholic thought. He also serves as director of the Envoy Institute of Belmont Abbey College.

Patrick has authored twelve books on Catholic themes, including *Pope Fiction: Answers to 30 Myths and Misconceptions About the Papacy, Search and Rescue: How to Bring Your Family and Friends Into, or Back Into, the Catholic Church* and *150 Bible Verses Every Catholic Should Know,* and has edited and coauthored the acclaimed multi-volume *Surprised by Truth* series, with over four hundred thousand combined copies in print, in English and Spanish. He is the host of four EWTN television and radio series as well as the Thursday edition of EWTN Radio's *Open Line* broadcast.

Patrick and his wife Nancy have been married for twenty-seven years and are blessed with eleven healthy and happy children and five grandchildren (who are also healthy and happy).

Patrick: The hard part when you invited me to speak about my most enduring spiritual experience was not to pick one thing but to pick *anything*. Quite honestly, and I'm serious about this, my spiritual life is by no means dramatic. I don't experience God in profound or dramatic or sudden ways, such as Saint Paul getting knocked off his horse. I've never been knocked off of anything, even a bicycle.

Al: Is it fair to say then that you were not "surprised by truth"?

Patrick: Not in the way you were—or the other converts in the *Surprised by Truth* books.[1] God always seems to work in my life in very subtle ways, and typically it's only in the rearview mirror that it suddenly dawns on me what it was that God was doing in my life.

But I do have a story to tell that's very important to me. I wrote about it in *Surprised by Truth 2* in my chapter "Conclusions of a Guilty Bystander."

I was working in sales in the late 1980s and was married to my beautiful wife, Nancy. We had four children, and I thought I was doing fine in my career. But over time I realized that I was growing more and more spiritually unsettled.

As my turmoil increased, I realized I was dealing with the reality of lukewarmness, being just a "Catholic on paper." Yes, I was Catholic—going to Mass on Sundays, saying grace before meals and praying occasionally—and if anyone asked what religion I was, I would immediately say, "Catholic." Intellectually and emotionally I loved the Catholic Church and had never been tempted to leave it. But I wasn't *living* like a Catholic in some areas of my life. I'm sorry to say that in some ways I was leading a more pagan lifestyle in terms of some of my attitudes and behavior. I had been lulled into a state of comfortable, "do not disturb" spiritual incapacitation. I lacked a deep interior commitment to Christ, to living virtuously and to deepening my prayer life.

Those things have a way of catching up with you. All people who have had some reckoning with God know this wave of repentance that can roll over you—out of nowhere, it seems. That's what happened to me. I realized it was time for some major changes.

Al: What kind of changes?

Patrick: Well, I was in this storm of turmoil about not having a fervent love for Jesus Christ, and though I was practicing my Catholic Faith, I knew that those sinful areas of my life had to be cleaned up and corrected. Because I was working in sales, I was able to go to a holy hour at a nearby parish on my lunch break. I went just about every weekday, spending an hour before the Blessed Sacrament, praying the rosary and, figuratively speaking, beating my head against the door of the tabernacle, asking the Lord to forgive me and strengthen and guide me. I also had this very deep and abiding sense that God wanted me to do something with my life, but I had no clue what it was.

One lunch hour I was praying before the Blessed Sacrament, skipping lunch as a minor mortification. For the first time I started to see my life in perspective: the time I had wasted, the frivolity, my sensuality, my years of compromise and complacency—they all accused me. Christ's words resonated in my soul: "Why do you call me 'Lord, Lord,' and not do what I tell you?" (Luke 6:46). A painful, tearful and very liberating wave of contrition washed over me, and a powerful new desire to be close to Christ filled me as never before.

Al: Sounds dramatic to me.

Patrick: It was very troubling actually. On one hand I had emerged from the crucible of my guilty conscience, remorse, self-reproach and repentance. On the other I still didn't know the next step. I still did not have a clue as to what God was calling me to do with my life.

Over the course of that month, I asked God in every way I knew how to show me what he wanted me to do. When I didn't see anything more clearly at the end of the month than I had at the beginning, I thought I would try to be like Simon and step out of the comfort zone of my little fishing boat by quitting my job (see Matthew 14:27–29). To this day I don't know what galvanized me to just quit, but I did.

I figured I should have some excuse for quitting my job, so I waited for my boss to look at me cross-eyed or do some silly thing and used that as a reason. I know that was a rather audacious and seemingly stupid thing to do. And I'm *very* fortunate that Nancy didn't whack me on the side of my head with a rolling pin. She must have had a special grace telling her to trust me and let me work this out however I felt I had to.

I figured I'd have a few weeks to sort out what my next step would be. But God didn't wait that long.

The next day was Saturday, and I was in the middle of contemplating what I was going to do with my life when a friend called on the phone. We had known each other for about a year, and we would talk every couple weeks. We shared a common interest in apologetics. We both liked to discuss the Faith and talk to Protestants, Mormons and other groups.

I told my friend, "Please pray for me, because I know God wants me to do something with my life, but I just don't know what it is."

Graciously he said, "I'll pray for you," and he added, "But I'll do something even better than that. I'm about to close down my law practice and do apologetics full-time. Why don't you come work with me, and we'll build this into something bigger than a one-man show?"

That friend, as I'm sure you know, Al, was Karl Keating.[2]

My first reaction was, "Thank you, but no." I had all kinds of grandiose ideas about what God might want me to do with my life, but working in the field of apologetics certainly wasn't one of them.

Nancy sweetly reminded me that I didn't have a job and suggested that maybe I should take this opportunity. On top of that, Karl was persistent. So I finally got the message through my thick skull and agreed to work with Karl at Catholic Answers on a trial basis. Several months later I finally realized that *this* was God's answer.

This took place over twenty years ago. I am so grateful to God and to Karl Keating for that fortuitous, life-changing phone call. I have to laugh at my own ridiculous reaction. Neither Karl nor I envisioned what Catholic Answers would one day become, with its international reach and its extraordinary influence on the apologetics revival going on in America.

The real power of this story is what Christ did for me in the Blessed Sacrament. Going to the Lord in the tabernacle and praying the rosary was the solution. When people ask me about problems in their lives, that's the advice I give them: Go to the Lord in the Blessed Sacrament! He will help you.

Russell Shaw
The Work of God, the Work of Life

Christ Jesus always did what was pleasing to the Father, *and always lived in perfect communion with him. Likewise Christ's disciples are invited to live in the sight of the Father "who sees in secret," in order to become "perfect as your heavenly Father is perfect."*
— *CCC*, 1693, quoting Matthew 6:6; 5:48; see John 8:29

Russell Shaw is Washington correspondent for *Our Sunday Visitor*. From the late sixties through the late eighties, he served as secretary of public affairs of the National Conference of Catholic Bishops. He is the author, coauthor or editor of numerous books, including *Papal Primacy in the Third Millennium* and *Our Sunday Visitor's Encyclopedia of Catholic Doctrine*. His twentieth book, *Nothing to Hide: Secrecy, Communication, and Communion in the Catholic Church*, was published in 2008.

Russell: I'm a cradle Catholic. I attended Catholic schools, grade school through graduate school. Throughout my overly long professional life, I have worked for institutions and organizations almost entirely associated with the Catholic Church. And almost all of my writing has been about Catholic themes. So I'm a pretty Catholic guy and have been for a long time.

But several decades ago, as I entered my forties, I was a mediocre Catholic—and that's a generous assessment. I did the bare minimum, spiritually speaking; I was no great shakes. And then something happened in April 1979 that made a big, big difference. A friend invited me to go on an Opus Dei[1] retreat.

Now, this friend, I should say parenthetically, was not then in Opus Dei, and he's not in Opus Dei now, and I'm sorry to say, he probably never will be. But somebody had asked him to go on this retreat, and he said yes. I think he wanted me to go along as moral support for him. So I said, OK, why not?

The retreat seemed to be going along pretty well, nothing sensational, and I was feeling comfortable. We had some free time on Saturday afternoon, so I was sitting in my room reading a book—not a very religious book, frankly—and I couldn't concentrate. As I perceived it, I was getting a message, for heaven's sake.

Now, I don't mean that I had a vision, and I didn't hear voices, and I didn't see any handwriting on the wall. But I was getting a rather distinct message, and that message, if I were to put it into words, was, "Your life is a disorderly mess. Pull up your socks, and get your act together."

Al: Whoa! What did you do with that?

Russell: The priest leading the retreat was a pretty good guy, and I continued seeing him for a few weeks after the retreat. Finally he said to me, "You know, I think the trouble with you is that you have a vocation to Opus Dei, and you don't know it." And it clicked; it just sounded right. I could see that he and the Holy Spirit had put their fingers on exactly what God wanted me to do at that point in my life.

So since 1979 I've been a member of Opus Dei, and I thank God for it. It's my particular vocation, highly rewarding and central to my attempts to live as an authentic Catholic.

Al: And you have not found any albino monks associated with Opus Dei?[2]

Russell: Very funny, Al.

Al: So has life been a smooth sail since 1979?

Russell: I have to say honestly that if anyone thinks that somebody in my situation doesn't have any problems or temptations or failings, they're wrong. I have all the weaknesses and problems that everybody else has. But what I've learned—and this is the central lesson for me—is that the essence of the interior life, or the attempt to have an interior life, a relationship with God, is to keep trying. Start over again every day. If you fall down, get up and try again. Persistence, perseverance, that's the key to it. You're not going to become a brand-new person overnight, but over a period of many years perhaps, God will lead you in his way to the fulfillment that he has in mind for you.

So I'm on the way. I'm making a journey, and I'm trying to get from here to there, and I'm somewhere at midpoint at the moment.

Al: Is your experience in Opus Dei rigorous?

Russell: After I began to understand the program and spirit of Opus Dei, I came to the conclusion that this is pretty much what anybody serious about living an authentic Catholic life would do: Mass and Communion every day, mental prayer every day, spiritual reading, reading the Holy Scriptures and so forth. So I don't regard it as rigorous. It sounds overwhelming when you come at it cold. But if you integrate these various elements of a spiritual program over the course of your life, they become second nature.

What's been very helpful, by the way, is having a routine, a plan of life, well-established spiritual practices that I try to incorporate into my life every single day. I don't get scrupulous about it, bent out of shape if I can't do something on a particular day. But these things serve as a norm and a guide to organizing my life.

Another big, big help is having a spiritual director, a reliable, sensible friend who can help and encourage me along the way. Now, a spiritual director is not going to be constantly dropping pearls of spiritual wisdom. Mainly he's a sounding board who can give good, common-sense reactions to my experiences and my questions. And I'm very grateful for that.

JOHN MARTIGNONI
It's Real!

> *The Eucharist is the memorial of Christ's Passover, the making present and the sacramental offering of his unique sacrifice, in the liturgy of the Church which is his Body.*
>
> —*CCC*, 1362

John Martignoni is a Catholic apologist and popular speaker. He hosts EWTN Global Catholic Radio's Monday *Open Line* program. He is also the founder and president of the Bible Christian Society, which offers free apologetics resources for Catholics. John also manages Queen of Heaven radio in Birmingham, Alabama.

John: Basically I was raised Catholic, left the faith when I went off to college and came back to the faith about thirteen years later. But when I returned to the Church, I was still what we would call a "cafeteria Catholic." I was pretty much uncatechized. Not knowing the rationale behind the Church's teachings, I rejected whatever I didn't want to believe.

Al: What were you doing for a living?

John: I was teaching finance at the University of North Alabama. It's a little regional university here in Florence, in Alabama's northwest corner. My schedule allowed me to go to daily Mass, and I really enjoyed being back in the Church.

Al: So what did God do to move you beyond the cafeteria?

John: I've never publicly shared this before, but here's what happened:

One Sunday—and on several subsequent Sundays over the next five or six months—I was in the Communion line, in twentieth-century Florence, Alabama, and all of a sudden I was "transported" through time and space to where I was a first-century Jew, hoeing my little vegetable garden outside of Jerusalem. I make no attempt to explain this. I make no claims that this was a "vision" or any such thing. But I do know that this was more than just a thought, because I could feel and experience with all five senses.

And as a first-century Jewish farmer, I was turning up the soil, and I heard a sound echo through the hills. It was the sound of metal hitting metal. I remember standing up, looking around, wondering what it was. My twentieth-century self knew it was the sound of the nails being hammered into Jesus' flesh.[1]

This caused an overwhelming feeling inside. It was everything I could do to keep from crying as I received Communion. And when I was back in my pew (after the first time this happened, I started sitting in the very back pew) I bowed my head as I knelt, and tears just rolled down my face. I just couldn't stop them.

Al: This experience continued in the same very tactile, full engagement of your senses?

John: Yes. It never happened during the weekday Mass, and it didn't happen every Sunday, but probably every other Sunday for about five or six months. And again I tell you that it wasn't a mere *thought*, because I can think about it now, and I don't have anywhere near the experience that I had when it actually happened.

Al: Do you mean you now have distance from it and can't reproduce it by recalling it?

John: Exactly. I can recreate the scene in my mind, but I don't really *feel* it. I don't hear the sound reverberating through the hills. It's completely different at an experiential level.

Al: Tell me more.

John: I kept going to daily Mass, and then came Holy Week. I had never been to a Holy Thursday Mass where the priest, in imitation of Christ, washes the feet of twelve members of the assembly. I was sitting in the back pew again, and when the priest went down for the foot washing, I had this incredible feeling of love for the Church. That's the moment when I fell in love with the Catholic Church.

It was that night that I realized that this Eucharist is really the Body, Blood, Soul and Divinity of Jesus Christ. And this Church really *is* the body of Christ. And it's real, it's so beautiful. My experience that night just put it all together for me.

After that Holy Thursday Mass, I never again experienced that sense of being transported back to the first century. It had been a gift from God to cement me to the Church and make me understand that going to church is no mere obligation. Christ is real; he's alive in the Eucharist. He comes now into our lives, just as truly as in the first century. Even though there are times when I don't have the *feeling* of Christ's real presence, those unusual experiences have cemented in my mind the *fact* that this is Jesus Christ.

Al: I don't want to put words into your mouth, but let me try to fathom the import of these remarkable experiences. The teaching that the Mass is a re-presentation of Christ's saving work on Calvary, that in the Mass we enter sacred time and are "transported" back to Calvary, that in the Eucharist Christ is our contemporary, all this was somehow infused into your consciousness during these experiences?

John: Yes. And this happened before I ever heard about apologetics and people like Scott Hahn and Tim Staples, or Catholic radio and EWTN. All that was foreign to me at the time. But this experience taught me that everything I was hearing, everything I was reading, everything I was seeing and experiencing within the Catholic Church is *real*. There's nothing symbolic about it; there's nothing that's merely nice or character-building about it. It's a real thing that's happening right now.

Al: Do you believe that this grace was given to you in preparation for the apostolic work that you're doing now?

John: Possibly so, because other things have happened to me, and I had no idea at the time how they were preparing me for future work. But now I look back and know exactly why they happened.

For example, when I was away from the Church, I worked for a defense contractor in Huntsville, Alabama. I was working on a project that involved a missile built by General Dynamics, the Stinger missile system. And it became necessary for me to go out to General Dynamics for a week and present all this research I had been doing.

I *hated* giving presentations in front of people. In college, when I had to do group presentations or individual presentations, my voice would wobble, my knees would shake, and "Uh, uh, bu...bu...bu...bu...bu..."—that's how I would talk. It was like jumping into a pool of my own sweat. So here I was, a twenty-six-year-old snot-nosed kid, flying out to meet with executive VPs who ran divisions with five, eight thousand people. I almost threw up on the plane.

The next morning—and I can't say I prayed about it because I was away from the Church—I had absolutely no fear. I went into that meeting and just blew 'em away. After that I never again feared public speaking.

At the time I really didn't think about this much. But now I look back, and I confess that it was preparing me for what I'm doing now.

So I think you're correct in concluding that the experience of being in first-century Jerusalem, near the crucifixion of Christ, *was* a preparation for what I'm doing now. When I talk to people, there's no doubt in any fiber of my being that what I'm telling them as Catholic teaching is the absolute truth, and that they need to listen if they want to improve their lives now and for the hereafter.

THREE

The Invisible Hand

- ●

- ●

- ●

- ●

- ●

- ●

There Are No Accidents

> *The witness of Scripture is unanimous that the solicitude of divine providence is* concrete *and* immediate; *God cares for all, from the least things to the great events of the world and its history.*
>
> —*CCC*, 303

Teresa Tomeo is a veteran broadcast journalist whose faith requires her to do more than report. She demands action. Truth requires response.

One of my first memories of Teresa is as a reporter for the ABC TV affiliate in Detroit. She'd been assigned to cover a fire that destroyed the St. Vincent de Paul Society's store, warehouse and distribution center on Detroit's East Side just before Christmas. As I watched her report, I noticed that she was exhorting her viewers to replace the losses as a sign of their commitment to Christmas. It was a notable departure from the detached, objective style characteristic of many TV reporters. Hers was a passionate professionalism.

For more than twenty years Teresa has served in radio and TV as reporter, news director and anchorperson. Her work has been recognized by the Associated Press, the Detroit Press Club and American Women in Radio and Television. She's a professional speaker, media consultant and my colleague as host of Ave Maria Radio's *Catholic Connection*. She recently authored *Noise: How Our Media-Saturated Culture Dominates Lives and Dismantles Families* and has also told her story in *Newsflash! My Surprising Journey from Secular Anchor to Media Evangelist.*

Teresa: God has hit me upside the head with two-by-fours several times; I guess I need that from time to time.

On October 15, 2004, the feast day of Saint Teresa of Avila—after whom I was named—my parents, Rose and Mike, had the accident that was no accident. God was so much at work in the circumstances that it became almost comical, although this was a very severe car crash. I've learned that when I get into a situation that is painful or confusing, the first thing to say is, "OK, Lord, if it's your will, I accept it." But most importantly I ask, "What do you want me to learn from this situation?"

Now, being Italian, we like to do things big, and so when my mother lost control of the car that evening, it was horrendous. She didn't just crash into one car; she crashed into four parked cars before smashing into the side of a restaurant, which we now conveniently call "Rosie's Drive-In." The amazing thing is that this happened in a very busy part of the east Detroit suburbs, at the corner of Mack and Eight Mile.

Al: It doesn't get much busier.

Teresa: It happened on a rainy, misty Friday evening, around 5:30. My mom and dad were coming home from their regular Friday night pizza. There are four lanes of traffic: two lanes north and two lanes south. My mother was trying to make a left-hand turn when she lost control of the vehicle. She sped across two lanes of northbound Mack, jumped a median and then crossed two lanes of southbound Mack, hitting four cars and smashing into a wall.

My father and mother were severely injured in the crash. The amazing thing is that no one else was hurt. With all that traffic and her crossing all those lanes, she hit only parked vehicles—no moving vehicles and no pedestrians. It was like the parting of the Red Sea.

Riding in the ambulance with my parents that night, I said to the Lord, "I don't understand why you would allow two people who are seventy-eight years old, just out on a pizza run, to get into this accident, but I'm sure you're going to show me."

The doctors examined Mom and Dad and did some tests, and we learned something that had never been detected before: My father had a silent heart disease. There were no signs—no high blood pressure, no pain, nothing. Had he not been in that accident, he could have dropped dead at any moment.

My parents were in the hospital for about three weeks recovering from their injuries. About a month later my father had open-heart surgery: a quadruple bypass and valve replacement. So that's number one in how I saw God at work.

The second lesson was that God's people are everywhere. There were so many great people involved at the scene, it's as though God planted them there. The police sergeant who handled the case was the brother of Monsignor Chuck Kosanke, one of my best friends. One of the cars my mother hit was owned by a fellow choir member, who was one of my dad's closest friends. It was comical!

Another lesson that came out of this "accident that was no accident" was one of reconciliation. At that particular time I was not speaking to my sister, who also lives in Michigan. She is strongly pro-choice, and I am strongly pro-life. She was very involved in the Jennifer Granholm and John Kerry campaigns.[1] We had to part ways because whenever we opened our mouths, we argued so much it disturbed our entire family.

My mom called me about the accident, and then I had to call my sister. She's a registered nurse, very intelligent, very competent. The Lord told me, "This night is not about politics." (We were just a few weeks before the presidential election of '04.) He said, "This is about being a sister and a daughter. Roll your sleeves up, shut your mouth and do what you've got to do." That night my sister came to the emergency room, and we spoke for the first time in months.

I think of that statement that is attributed to Saint Francis, "Speak the gospel always; use words if necessary." And I think my and my husband Dominic's presence every single day at the hospital, caring for my parents, coming together with my sister and doing what was necessary, was itself a witness to Christ. My sister probably thought, "Gosh, maybe they actually take this Christian stuff seriously." And even though we still don't agree on issues, we have a much better relationship today. We're even talking!

I see the beginning of a restored relationship as one of the things that God was directly saying to me: "Look, you still have to be a sister. Yes, you must be faithful in defending the unborn, but sometimes you can only witness by your actions."

Al: Have you had a chance to talk to your mom and dad about the significance of their experience?

Teresa: Yes. My mom breaks down every time she talks about it, because it was uncanny that she didn't hit anybody. I mean, there are two or three restaurants, an ice cream parlor, a gas station, loads of pedestrian traffic, whole families walking in and out of those places. And then, of course, the traffic on Eight Mile and Mack! Sometimes a pedestrian has to wait five minutes to cross Mack. So the fact that she didn't hit anybody reduces her to tears of gratitude.

God must have a sense of humor too, because the cars Mom did hit were already in for repair. An auto repair shop keeps a lot right next to the restaurant that they ran into. So when she crossed southbound Mack Avenue, she hit the cars parked there for repair before she went into the wall of the restaurant.

Al: When the veil is pulled aside, we see that behind these events God is really at work, achieving his purposes in our lives. In this instance he's doing the work of family reconciliation. He's doing the work of conforming you to Christ. He's doing the work of medical diagnosis in your dad's case.

Teresa: Yeah, it was physical and spiritual healing for our family. My mother woke up from her morphine-induced state, saw my sister and me standing at the foot of her bed and said in her "Joisey" accent—which she's never lost, even though we've lived here for over forty years—"Oh, my goodness! This is why this accident happened, so you and your sistah could tawk again." And then she dropped right back to sleep.

The doctors said that my dad's surgery, which we would not have discovered a need for had that accident not happened, probably added ten years to his life.

So God is good all the time, even in the midst of a horrendous accident that was no accident.

PAUL THIGPEN

From Optimism to Hope

Whether we realize it or not, prayer is the encounter of God's thirst with ours. God thirsts that we may thirst for him.
—*CCC*, 2560; see Saint Augustine, *De diversis quaestionibus octoginta tribus* 64, 4: PL 40, 56

octor Paul Thigpen is professor of theology at Southern Catholic College in Dawsonville, Georgia. He is also editor of *The Catholic Answer*, a national bimonthly magazine published by Our Sunday Visitor. A best-selling author, award-winning journalist and scholar of Church history, he has published thirty-five books in a wide variety of genres.

Paul graduated from Yale University in 1977 *summa cum laude*, Phi Beta Kappa, with distinction in the major of religious studies. He was later awarded the Robert W. Woodruff Fellowship at Emory University in Atlanta, where he earned an M.A. (1993) and a PH.D. (1995) in historical theology.

Paul is a lover of place. He has graciously led me around his hometown, Savannah, more than once, regaling me with history lessons, theological meditations, social commentary and ghost stories. He has almost persuaded me that Savannah is America's most beautiful and intriguing city.

Paul: A lot of folks who know me may be surprised to find out that as a teenager I was an atheist. Though I had been raised in a Christian home, at about the age of twelve I began reading Voltaire and other Enlightenment[1] thinkers. Between those skeptical influences and the fact that I was a rebellious adolescent who wanted to reject the values of my parents, I became an atheist.

Al: How long did your atheism continue?

Paul: This went on until I was eighteen. Then God did some amazing things to turn me around.

I grew up in beautiful Savannah, Georgia, and live there now. The day I was born, the newspaper headlines across the country read, "Schools must integrate." The Supreme Court, in *Brown* v. *Board of Education,* had determined that so-called "separate but equal" systems of education for blacks and whites were unconstitutional. Savannah only began implementing that decision when I was seventeen.

During my sophomore year I became one of the first white students to attend what had been an all-black high school. The authorities knew full desegregation was coming, so they offered a "freedom of choice" plan: A student could choose a school with a different majority color. I quite agreeably went to a black school along with a number of my friends. We had a great time for two years getting to know folks across racial lines.

This "social experiment" validated my atheistic, optimistic humanism. I was convinced, like a good little Enlightenment boy several centuries too late, that all we needed to perfect us was the right education and social influence.

Al: So ignorance, not sin, was the great obstacle to human flourishing.

Paul: Exactly. Those first two years in the black high school, I was an activist in student government and clubs. I said, "OK, I'm going to help my black friends get to know my white friends and my white friends get to know my black friends." We just needed knowledge of one another.

My school's little experiment turned out well, and during my senior year, 1971–1972, the school board mandated a certain percentage of black and white students in *all* city schools. Residential districts were divided up and students shuffled all over town. A number of extremely militant white and black students were assigned to my school, while many of my friends, black and white, were moved to other schools.

That fall racial conflict exploded in the schools. Most of the high schools decided to forgo electing a homecoming queen. They thought that forcing a choice between black and white girls would be volatile. A couple of the schools offered a feeble compromise: "OK, we'll elect a black homecoming queen and a white one."

My school had been without racial incident until then. We were confident that peace would continue. As student body president I declared, "This is ridiculous; we will not institutionalize this kind of racism." So with adolescent hubris I led the push to select a single homecoming queen.

On homecoming day I didn't know that a half mile away another high school had already been closed by rioting. Black and white militants from that school came onto our campus, infiltrated our pep rally and hooted at the candidates of opposite color. As we left the assembly, one guy pushed another down from behind, and then others piled on him. Right in front of my eyes, a riot erupted. Chains, knives and tire irons came out; it was just horrible.

The instigators of the riot had drifted over from another campus. I thought my classmates, my "kin," were still pure. But right in front of me, I saw some of my close friends and acquaintances out to kill each other. I was pulling people off each other. My watch was knocked off my arm and crushed.

In that one moment everything that I had done as a student leader for those three years crumbled in front of me. All it took was a touch of irrational stupidity. Things would never be the same again. It was so *unreasonable*, so *unenlightened*.

I dragged myself—stunned—back to the classroom of a favorite teacher, who was a Christian. Tears welled up, and I bawled my eyes out—just wailed. Chaos had been unleashed. I'm sure some students went to the hospital, though nobody was seriously injured.

It was the end of my "enlightened religion." For weeks I was in a kind of spiritual stupor. Then a most amazing thing happened.

Although I was an atheist, I had some Christian friends. One of them, Rita, was walking with me to class one day. The school was kind of ranch style from the fifties, designed in wings and not very big. We were walking between two wings, and we could see in a field between the wings a huge mob, with blacks on one side and whites on the other. Furious faces, clenched fists, weapons in hand, they faced off against each other.

I could tell what was going to happen. When a mob reached that point of fury and reaction, there was no turning back. Even the arrival of the police wouldn't avert a riot. Six or eight feet away from each other, both sides were ready to rumble.

Rita looked at me and said, "I don't know about you, but the only thing to do is pray." And right there on the sidewalk, she dropped to her knees and began to implore God to intervene. (I still can't tell this story without getting choked up.)

I didn't know what else to do, so I also knelt and said, "Whew, God (if there is a God), this can't be your will. You can't let this happen."

No sooner had we prayed than a spirit of laughter fell on the mob. I don't know what else to call it. The group went from utter fury to an irrational and contagious hilarity. People started laughing, and the people alongside them started laughing, and the people on the other side started laughing. Within sixty seconds they were all laughing. They put away their weapons, turned around and went to class.

Al: How did you explain it?

Paul: I couldn't. Nobody could. Afterward I talked to some of the students. Why were they laughing? "We don't know. Everybody else was laughing, and who can fight when you're laughing?"

To this day I'm moved by the memory. I was far from embracing all the nuances of Christian faith: the Trinity, the Incarnation, the mystery of redemption. But that day, for the first time, in my heart I could say: "There is a God, and he cares."

Al: You were not a praying boy. Did you feel sheepish?

Paul: I was an atheist, so yes, I felt sheepish, but I didn't care. I couldn't stand to see my friends and community get hurt again, especially knowing how it could escalate. I was willing to try anything, and when Rita fell to her knees, I fell in right beside her and prayed, "God (if there is a God), you can help." And he did.

Al: How long before you took the next step and decided to follow Jesus?

Paul: By the end of my senior year I believed that Jesus was Lord. Other prayers had been answered. Scripture had impressed itself on my spiritual imagination. God brought these things and others together to form truly Christian convictions within me.

But he knew I first had to become disillusioned with my silly secular religion. I had to lose my optimistic, atheistic innocence. We cannot save ourselves. We cannot create a world of peace, justice and harmony without his plan and power.

Al: It's a powerful image: those two groups facing off against each other, and there are you and Rita falling on your knees. The wall of unbelief came down.

Paul: By this time I had had some occult experiences and had come to believe that there was something beyond just matter and energy, something beyond the reach of science. But when God answered Rita's and my prayer, it was so remarkable. Not a physical miracle, but my goodness, as to what it meant to me, it had the impact similar to a resurrection from the dead. It meant so much to me to see my friends saved from devastation.

Al: Not only saved but erupting in laughter.

Paul: That was the other thing: What a wild way for it to happen. If a helicopter full of police had come down and somehow stopped the fight, OK, that would have been an answer to prayer. But the laughter was such a remarkable way for it to happen. How could you explain it except as an answer to prayer? It was stunning.

Al: Did you come to see Christ and his Church as fulfilling your ideal of community? Or did you reject the ideal?

Paul: I didn't reject the ideal. I probably would have been on my way to bitterness if God hadn't moved in on me. At the end of the year, I met some Christians who shared that ideal of a harmonious community—not just among races but also among all kinds of folks, male and female, rich and poor, educated and uneducated. Then I became involved with a biracial Christian church that shared a genuine love and care that I had never seen before.

When I went off to college, the Yale Christian Fellowship was composed of all kinds of colors and backgrounds. And I realized, "Here it is. I've been transformed, these people have been transformed individually, and together we really are part of a new community."

Al: It wasn't just the work of human organization or conflict resolution skills.

Paul: No! Nor was it economics or politics. The people who lived in harmony still experienced inequities and prejudices, but by the Spirit of God they rose above those things and became one in Christ.

CHRIS GODFREY
Who's Calling This Play?

> *God is the sovereign master of his plan. But to carry it out he also makes use of his creatures' cooperation.*
>
> —*CCC*, 306

When I met Chris Godfrey, he was on his knees. Nearly fifteen years ago, as a few friends and I were passing an abortion clinic on M-39 in Southfield, Michigan, we saw a strong young man bent over on the sidewalk, in a posture of prayerful petition. Fingering his rosary beads, Chris could have been posing as a type of Christian Atlas shouldering the burden of all the pain and moral evil that had passed through those wailing walls. He had heard Rachel crying for her children, and he was her Jacob wrestling with an angel to bring a blessing out of brutality (see Jeremiah 31:15; Matthew 2:18; Genesis 32:22–31).

We stopped to join Chris in prayer, and I learned that he had played in the National Football League (NFL) for nine years. He was the starting right guard for the Super Bowl XXI (1986) champion New York Giants. He also played on three University of Michigan Rose Bowl teams. After leaving the NFL he attended and graduated from the University of Notre Dame Law School.

Chris has authored the popular curricula *That's Where I Live: A Guide to Good Relationships*, *Mike and Will's Not-So-Excellent Adventure*, *As in a Mirror* and the *See I Make All Things New* series. While still in the NFL, Chris founded Life Athletes, Inc., of which he remains the president. He resides in South Bend, Indiana, with his wife and six children and is a member of the Indiana bar.

Chris: I was one year out of college and in my first year in the NFL when I had a series of adventures or misadventures in which God really got my attention.

Al: He didn't have it already? Weren't you raised Catholic?

Chris: I had the benefit of being born and raised in a Catholic family, attending Catholic grade school and high school. I received great training and lots of love. But when I got into my teen years and into college, God drifted off my radar screen. In that sense mine's not an unusual story for a young man.

I wasn't denying God or defiantly turning my back on him. I just got busy. My horizons were broadening, my opportunities were increasing, and more and more freedom was becoming mine. I did notice, however, that as I grew further and further away from God, I was growing sadder on the inside.

Al: How long did this drifting continue?

Chris: It wasn't until I got into the NFL that all of that changed.

The NFL draft had finished over the weekend, and unfortunately, I hadn't been drafted. I did, however, sign a free-agent contract with the Washington Redskins. Nobody gave me much of a chance to make the team that year, because they had brought in over a hundred new guys to fill only forty-five spots, and most of those spots were already taken by guys returning from the previous year. So just the top draft picks would be kept. The rest of us were there to make the lines longer for the veterans, so they could rest between drills.

But little by little I gained the coach's attention. Even the media began talking about my likely prospects. During my last preseason game at the old RFK Stadium, I sacked the quarterback, and a sack really draws attention to a defensive lineman.

Afterward I was driving around in my buddy's moon-roofed Mercedes, listening to the postgame commentator talking about what a great pass rusher I was and how I was going to make the team that year. I just kicked back thinking, "Yeah, I sure can get used to living like this."

Everyone wanted to talk to me. I didn't have to buy anything; everything was paid for. I was a Redskin, and I made a conscious decision to just let go and enjoy the so-called good life in the nation's capital.

But God had other plans. The next day I was in the training room getting my ankles taped for the game. The assistant coach walked in and told me that the head coach wanted to see me. And, "Oh, yeah, bring your playbook."

"Bring" meant "turn in." Sure enough, I was cut. I was shocked, and everyone in the training room was shocked too.

A couple weeks later the New York Giants picked me up, and I spent the season backing up the famous "New York Sack Exchange"—Joe Klecko, Marty Lyons, Mark Gastineau and Abdul Salaam.[1] The next year, the day before I came up for training camp, I injured my knee in a freak accident. So I couldn't practice; a week later they cut me.

I returned home to Detroit, a fourteen-hour drive from Hofstra University, where the Giants practiced. A note was sitting on my mom's kitchen table from the Green Bay Packers, inviting me to their training camp the next day. Rather than get excited, I was close to saying, "Forget it. I've been doing this too long."

Al: You'd been through this before.

Chris: Exactly. Maybe it was time for me to get a "real" job.

But to my surprise the Packers had just signed the Redskins coach who had worked with me the previous year. We had become friends, and I trusted that he wouldn't waste my time. So I went up to Green Bay, and fair enough, they told me that I made the team! I finally let myself welcome a rush of enthusiasm.

I called home and talked to my dad, my sisters and my girlfriend, who is now my wife. They dropped everything, brought my car and clothes up to Green Bay and stayed for the last Packers preseason game at Lambeau Field. They went home the next day. And the next morning I got a wake-up call from an assistant coach *telling me I was cut*—for the third time in a year.

I hung up the phone and, without even thinking, dropped to my knees and prayed: "Lord, I give up. Whatever you want me to do, wherever you want me to go, you're the boss now."

I'd never really prayed like that before. I always had another plan up my sleeve. I was probably like a lot of people who, whenever they have a decision to make between doing something their way or doing something God's way, usually find a way to rationalize doing it their way. That had been my way of playing the divine guidance game.

But this prayer was different. Now I wanted to do the Lord's will in the Lord's way. So, anchored in my prayer and accepting, even resigned to, the will of God, I packed up my bags, headed out of the hotel, went across the street to Lambeau Field and cleared out my locker.

That's when Head Coach Bart Starr[2] called me into his office and apologized for cutting me. Would I stay on? This was unheard of. I'd been around the NFL long enough to know that top-tier coaches don't make mistakes of this sort. Every play is filmed, and every night the coaches talk about who the lucky few are going to be.

At that moment I knew that God was near.

Al: Unbelievable.

Chris: Yes. And because God had drawn close to me, I immediately wanted to move closer to him.

This is my most enduring spiritual lesson: God is close. I constantly go back to this lesson, especially when I am thinking deeply about things. Remembering this experience is almost like reading a favorite Scripture passage: I always find something new in it. I find that's the case with that whole turn of events.

Many years later, when I was with the New York Giants and had won Super Bowl XXI, Bart Starr came to one of our dinners. The dinner was hosted by our team chaplain, Father Ken Moore, now deceased, who was a Carmelite. It was his brother who had given the legendary Vince Lombardi[3] his first job at St. Cecilia High School in New Jersey. Bart Starr, of course, was Vince Lombardi's quarterback during the Packers' glory days. So there's another of those inscrutable "coincidences."

From Bart Starr I learned how all the behind-the-scenes decision making had worked. It was kind of neat to bring it together in that way.

MARCUS GRODI

Our God Is a Sovereign God

> *Drawn from nothingness by God's power, wisdom, and good-*
> *ness, [the creature] can do nothing if it is cut off from its ori-*
> *gin, for "without a Creator the creature vanishes."*
> —*CCC*, 308, quoting *Gaudium et Spes*, 36 §3

Marcus Grodi is a former Presbyterian pastor who received his master of divinity degree from Gordon-Conwell Theological Seminary in South Hamilton, Massachusetts. Marcus's warmth, hospitality, biblical insight and evangelistic zeal have created the Coming Home Network International (CHNI), of which he is president and executive director. CHNI provides fellowship, encouragement and support for Protestant pastors and laymen who are somewhere along the journey into or have already been received into the Catholic Church.

Marcus hosts *The Journey Home* on EWTN and *Deep in Scripture* on EWTN Global Catholic Radio. He authored the novel *How Firm a Foundation* and edited *Journeys Home*.

Marcus: When it comes to stories, I'm often reminded of incidents in the life of Jesus. A number of times after he heals people, he warns them, "Don't tell anybody." New Testament scholars and theologians refer to this as the "messianic secret."[1] The thought is that Jesus didn't want more people to know about him than necessary, so he could continue his ministry.

But I've always had a different view. Sometimes when God touches our lives, it is simply for us, and it loses the power in the telling. God touches us in little ways all the time to awaken us to his love and mercy, but it's really for us and not necessarily for public sharing.

One little goofy story concerns my contact lenses. I was skiing up at Caberfae Peaks Ski Resort, about a hundred miles northwest of Grand Rapids, Michigan. I was at the top of the most difficult slope on a bright snowy day. I accidentally bumped my head with my ski pole, and both contacts popped out! I got down on my knees, looking and praying, "O Lord Jesus, you've got to help me find those contacts!" And I found them.

Now, the point is that I knew in that moment, almost like an infused reality, that this was the mercy of God. That's an example of a story that might not touch some people. They might be blind to the presence of God in the little everyday items of our lives. On the other hand, even stories like these might impart the grace of God and open hearts and minds.

All of that is prologue. Here's the story I want to tell: Maybe it won't touch anyone, but boy, I tell ya, it touched me!

I used to work as a plastics engineer for Dow Chemical Company in Midland, Michigan. My project was to develop "the best butter tub that ever existed."

I went to visit my parents in Perrysburg, Ohio, near Toledo, for a weekend and stayed far too late. I decided to stay overnight on Sunday, get up early on Monday and drive back to Midland. I was due back at work at 9:00 AM.

I arose at maybe 2:00 or 3:00 AM and started driving north. I was getting tired, and as I drove along Route 23, past Ann Arbor, I started to fall asleep at the wheel. I got off at an exit, grabbed a cup of coffee, put the driver's window down so that the cold air could whip my face, let my arm hang out the window and prayed, "Lord, please help me!" I was having a hard time.

At that moment a couple voices or promptings, or whatever you want to call them, said, "Number one, close that window. Number two, get your seatbelt on."

So I was driving north, trying to stay awake. At some point I had to get off the highway and onto a two-lane road. I was driving around sixty-five miles an hour. The next thing I remembered was that my Dodge Ram Charger was bouncing along the side of a semi-trailer. My first thought was to pull my car to the side of the road.

I did that, but I couldn't open my car door. I was nervous. What had happened to the other driver? I leaned back and kicked the door open, tore off my seatbelt and ran toward the truck.

The driver met me in the middle of the road, because he was wondering the same thing about me. We started laughing hard, out of nervousness.

I had fallen completely asleep at the wheel but was sitting upright, driving on his side of the road. He thought I was playing chicken at 4:00 in the morning, so at first he wasn't going to move. After all, he had the semi. He finally realized that this wasn't right. He turned the cab of his truck to the right and tried to whip the trailer out of my way.

I woke up when I hit the side of his truck and then followed the side of that truck all the way down. The entire left side of my own truck was pushed in about nine inches, and I had lost the mirror, yet I walked away without a scratch.

Al: Your arm was still on your shoulder?

Marcus: Yes, thanks to the fact that I had closed the window. And I was in my seatbelt. As I went back to the car and waited for the tow truck, I knew for sure that the only reason I was still alive was the grace of God. I should never have walked away from that. That was his mercy touching my life.

My life has never been the same from that moment, because I was absolutely convinced that whatever life I had left was his. I had no right to be alive.

That moment led me to reevaluate my job at Dow, and within two years I was in seminary. Within a couple years I was pastoring a Presbyterian church. Another few years and I was Catholic. A few more years and Mother Angelica had a crazy notion to let me do TV.

I look back on that incident to recognize that every single one of us is alive today because of the mercy of God. I was completely out of control and in the hands of my Lord Jesus Christ. And so to this day I know that I want to do whatever I can with my life, with the time that I have, for his glory.

Al: Whew, what's that song, "Jesus, Take the Wheel"? Do you often think back to that moment?

Marcus: Yes, but I have a long list of moments. Once I was held hostage in a bank robbery with a sawed-off shotgun to my head.

Al: Well, that certainly clarifies the mind and arranges priorities.

Marcus: I almost hate to mention this other event, because now my TV viewers may notice that one of my eyebrows sticks up higher than the other. I don't do that on purpose. When I was eight years old, I fell off a high diving board, hit my head on the side of the pool and was unconscious for several days. Again, I'm alive because of God's mercy.

Al: Marcus, remind me to never drive, bank or swim with you! Lord, have mercy.

Marcus: I really was asleep at the wheel, but there are a lot of people walking around very much awake but kind of asleep at the wheel because they don't recognize how much their lives depend on the constant grace and providence of God.

Al: Not everyone responds in faith as you did. How do we know if we have authentic faith credentials?

Marcus: Saint John asks that in his first letter: "How do you know that you know God?" You stand back, and you see that you actually love someone; you love someone because of God's grace, because you've been changed. You see that you are being obedient to the commands of God. But it isn't you; it's God at work within you (see 1 John 2:3–11; 4:7–18).

I gave that earlier example of finding the contacts on the side of the slope. In my heart that was as much a message of God's mercy as being saved in the truck accident. I could have said, "Boy, ain't I lucky?" But no, my knee-jerk response was, "Thank you, Lord Jesus." And that is proof to me that I've been changed. It's not me; it's his grace.

Al: You instinctively gave thanks. Good test. Do you talk to people who, in these situations, don't acknowledge the hand of God but eventually do—ten, fifteen, twenty years later? Or does this realization dawn during the moment?

Marcus: One thing I have found, especially when I talk with converts, is that they look back over the years and see places where God touched them.

Let me tell you an incident that happened not long before my father died, about three years ago. I love my father dearly, and I miss him very much, but I thank my Lord for the communion of saints, because I know he is still very close to me.

My father spent his last four years dying of emphysema. He was tied down with the oxygen tubes, and his life was bounded only as far as those oxygen tubes could reach. And so it consisted of the bedroom, the bathroom and the kitchen. I bought him a computer and set it up in the kitchen, and that became the main way we would communicate.

My father was not a practicing Christian. Most of my adult life he didn't go to church. His comment when I became Catholic was, well, if he ever became a Christian, he'd be Catholic. He always had a high view of Catholics; Saint Thomas More was his hero.[2]

My father became a steady viewer of the *Journey Home* program. However, we never could talk about the faith. It was that father-son thing. But e-mail opened us up. We could talk in e-mail.

One day I wrote him a long letter, charitably challenging his faith because I recognized that his life was reaching the end. He wrote me this wonderful letter back, saying, "You know, Marc, I do pray the Lord's Prayer, and I listen to what you and others say, and I appreciate that." But "the problem is, I'm not convinced that God wants me. I am not convinced that he loves me. I am not convinced that he hears me. I am not convinced that my prayers go anywhere. And truth be told, I really don't even know if I know how to pray." And then he wrote, "I'm getting tired, I've got to go back to bed. Love, Dad."

Well, I was going to answer him right away, but I got busy. The next morning I came to my office, turned on my computer, and there's an e-mail waiting for me. It's my dad, and he wrote, "God spoke to me." He said, "You remember yesterday I wrote you that e-mail saying I didn't know whether God loved me and whether he hears me or even if I know how to pray? Well, I left the kitchen, went back to the bedroom, laid down and picked up the book I happened to be reading."

My dad was an avid reader. He read every day of his life. At this time he was reading John Grisham's *The Testament*.[3] It's a story about a lawyer who goes to South America looking for a lost person and meets a missionary. My dad picked it up right where he had quit reading, and in the very first paragraph the lawyer was telling the missionary that he really didn't know if God loved him and he didn't how to pray.

My dad was nailed! He knew at that moment that this was no coincidence; it was God.

FOUR

One Small Step

•

•

•

•

•

•

SISTER ANN SHIELDS
God's Power Is Made Perfect in Weakness

For you love all things that exist, and detest none of the things that you have made; for you would not have made anything if you had hated it. How would anything have endured, if you had not willed it?... You spare all things, for they are yours, O Lord, you who love the living.

—Wisdom 11:24–26, as quoted in *CCC*, 301

Sister Ann Shields is a member of the Servants of God's Love, a Catholic religious order within the diocese of Lansing, Michigan. She hosts Renewal Ministries' daily radio program *Food for the Journey*, which offers enthusiastic, insightful reflections on the readings of the day. The love and wisdom expressed in *Food for the Journey* endows Sister Ann with a rare, understated moral authority: When Sister Ann speaks, people listen. My wife and daughter have demonstrated that, in a choice between Sister Ann's opinion and mine, I am the loser, or rather, they are the gainers.

Sister Ann has served on the National Service Committee of the Catholic Charismatic Renewal and is a prominent speaker at national and international conferences. She has authored four books, including *Intercession: A Guide to Effective Prayer* and *Deeper Conversion: Extraordinary Grace for Ordinary Times.*

Sister Ann: I'd like to share a two-part story of how God acted in my life.

I entered a religious community in 1957 and made final vows in 1965. We all know what 1965 was like: the end of the Second Vatican Council[1] and a time of great ferment in Church and society. In the two to three years after I took my final vows, many of my dearly held ideas were mocked, ridiculed and torn apart in both the Church and the world.

I was a very idealistic young woman who wanted to serve God with all her heart, soul, mind and strength. I didn't really have a voice and didn't even know how to find a voice in the face of what I was seeing. It was a very confusing time, internally as well as externally.

Al: Even for a religious who had made final vows?

Sister Ann: Exactly. Many sisters were trying to find their ground in a lot of wrong places. We were offered free courses in Silva Mind Control, avant-garde therapies and various New Age practices. As I said, it was a *very* confusing time.

I experienced severe depression. I knew that I loved God and wanted to serve him, but I hadn't discovered what I cherish now—a deeply personal relationship with God. He was somewhere out there, and I was here. I had a very simple faith, a very real faith, but holding on to that became very challenging for me.

On a very dreary February day, after two or three years of this crisis, I was standing by the window of our Pennsylvania convent. I didn't even know how to articulate a prayer. I remember resting my head against a window and just crying out, "Lord, if you really exist, please do something, just do something."

Then something very strange occurred. I turned and took two steps away from the window, and it was literally as if I walked into a person's chest. That's the experience I had. I thought, "Uh-oh. I have really lost it."

I stepped back and couldn't see anything. I took another two steps forward, and again, it was just as if there were a block there. I stopped, and then I heard, inaudibly but very clearly, "Don't you know I've been with you all the time?"

None of my questions were answered. None of my dilemmas were resolved. But in that moment I clearly knew that I was not alone. He was with me.

Al: Did you experience an immediate shift in your emotions?

Sister Ann: In every way. I still struggled with issues and concerns and people. I was seeing their sin and my sin in that struggle. Anger, bitterness and frustration can well up inside you when you're trying to articulate something and you just aren't clear about it, even in your own mind. I was fighting to understand myself as well as trying to make myself understood to others. That battle went on for probably three more years. But from that moment in February, I never doubted that there was a God or that he was with me.

Al: It was a whole new world.

Sister Ann: Yes, a new world. I was still floundering and searching for several years, probably well into 1970. But I could go ahead and live my life and try to find my way through things. I wasn't immobilized.

Al: When was the next turning point?

Sister Ann: In 1970 I was living in a convent with a sister in her late sixties who was dying of heart failure. She had been very, very good to me in my religious life, especially in those years of difficulty. One day, out of the blue, when I came home from teaching high school, she said, "Sister, there's a prayer meeting at the seminary this Friday night."

Now, it was a Pennsylvania December, with lots of snow. The trip would be twenty-seven miles up a mountain, and the snow would be heavier the closer we got to the prayer meeting. I didn't want to go, but she had been so good to me. So I said, "Sure, Sister."

The prayer meeting was not impressive. A group of about forty people gathered, many of them college professors and seminary faculty. They didn't know what they were doing. I didn't know what they were doing. They talked, they reflected, they prayed a bit, they sang—badly. I just sat through it, not at all inspired.

Finally it was over, and we drove the twenty-seven miles down the mountain, and that was that. "Don't let her ask me again," I hoped.

The following Wednesday Sister came to me and said, "I would love to go to that prayer meeting again." And I thought, "Why?" But she was committed. So again, twenty-seven miles up the mountain and twenty-seven miles down.

I took Sister there a few more times. One time we were stranded in a snowstorm on a ridge, and the state police had to direct one car down at a time. We didn't get home until three o'clock in the morning. But not once did I feel that I could say no to this sister; she had been so kind to me.

Al: Did the meetings get any better?

Sister Ann: After the second meeting a seminarian stopped me and asked, "Sister, what did you think?"

I said, "I don't know. I'm not thinking too much about it. I teach high school; it's the end of the week; I'm tired, you know. I just brought Sister."

So he said, "Well, I hope you come back."

I said, "Well, we'll see."

I took Sister to another prayer meeting in January, and again this seminarian approached me. "Sister, what did you think?"

In all my time at these meetings, nothing had touched me as my experience back in 1967 had. But after that meeting I thought, "These people seem to relate to God as though he were personal, as though God loved them. Could it be that what these people are looking for is what I'm looking for?" I just tucked this thought away in the back of my mind.

The next morning I woke up thinking that I really needed to get together with a friend who was a cloistered Carmelite. I hadn't talked with her for thirteen years.

Now, you don't just ring up cloistered Carmelite sisters, but I called and actually got hold of her. She told me to come over. What I didn't know was that Father Michael Scanlan[2] was the rector of the seminary at which the prayer meetings were held, his seminarians had been praying for me, and they had sent word to these sisters to pray for me.

My friend and I met in a room with a grille between us, and we prayed. We had prayed for about twenty-five minutes when she said to me, "What do you *really* want?"

I said, "This makes no sense, but I want to give my life to God in a way I never have before. He's been a clear presence that's brought comfort and strength, and I'm grateful. I've given my whole life to God already: I've taken vows of poverty, chastity and obedience. But I'm feeling a call to give more, and I don't know what that is. What more do I have to give?"

My Carmelite friend said, "Why don't you just tell God that?"

So I said, "Lord, here I am. I don't know what to say, except that I want to give my life to you in a way I never have before, and I don't know what that means."

At this point there was a knock on the door, and a sister came to tell me that my ride home was there, and so I left. It was that abrupt.

The next day I came home very tired from directing a high school play. I dragged myself into the chapel. I found myself saying (and these words are indelibly imprinted in my mind), "If you heard me yesterday, would you please do something to let me know you're here? Please. I'm just weak. It's not that I don't know you're here. I do, but please just give some sign, something that shows you've heard my prayers, some understanding that you accept my life at this level that even I don't understand."

I couldn't articulate it any better than that. I came out of the convent chapel and started up the stairs to a stack of English compositions awaiting my corrections.

If I went back to that convent today, I could tell you the exact step I was standing on when I felt as if somebody had taken a pitcher of water—only it was a pitcher of joy—that soaked me from the tip of my head to the soles of my feet. I was filled with joy, and I knew what that joy was: that God loved me and gave himself for me. Those words just kept going round and round in my head: "I love you. I gave myself for you."

I was so startled. And that joy has never gone. For the past thirty-seven years, the joy has been there all the time, the joy that God loves each of us and is always with us. My awareness of it has sometimes been low, sometimes circumstances are difficult and challenging, but that river of joy remains steady in my life.

Finding True Freedom

"Although he was a Son, [Jesus] learned obedience through what he suffered." How much more reason have we sinful creatures to learn obedience—we who in him have become children of adoption.

—*CCC*, 2825, quoting Hebrews 5:8

Joseph Pearce is the author of many literary studies of nineteenth- and twentieth-century Christian writers, including G.K. Chesterton, Aleksandr Solzhenitsyn, Hilaire Belloc, J.R.R. Tolkien, Oscar Wilde and C.S. Lewis. His *Literary Converts: Spiritual Inspiration in an Age of Unbelief* remains a classic demonstration of the inescapable link between spirituality, style and story. His recent *The Quest for Shakespeare: The Bard of Avon and the Church of Rome* reveals England's greatest writer in a devout Catholic family, defiant during persecution and dying a faithful Catholic.

Joseph is also the coeditor of the *St. Austin Review* and general editor of the Ignatius Critical Editions of the great books of Western culture. He is writer in residence and professor of literature at Ave Maria University in Florida.

In many happy hours of conversation with Joseph, I have been immersed in the sacramental imagination of the Church. Few men better grasp the culturally transforming power of the Christ who is the object of our faith. Fewer still are those whose lives are more passionately dedicated to helping others so grasp.

Joseph: My most enduring spiritual lesson is summarized in the phrase used by bodybuilders: "No pain, no gain." The moments of the greatest suffering in my life have been, paradoxically, the moments that have led to my greatest spiritual growth.

The first major suffering that led me closer to Mother Church took place during my second term in prison, before I was a believing Christian. I was very anti-Catholic. In fact, I was a racist.

When I was fifteen I had gotten involved in the National Front, a white-supremacist organization in England. We called for the compulsory repatriation of all nonwhite immigrants, such as Indians and Pakistanis. I joined the Orange Order, a pseudo-Masonic group whose sole purpose is to oppose "popery." Irish Republican Army terrorists killed two of my friends.

Many Englishmen still see Catholicism as a foreign religion incompatible with being a true Englishman. That was also part of the backdrop of my anti-Catholicism.

I had already been convicted once for publishing material likely to incite racial hatred. This second conviction brought me a twelve-month prison sentence.[1] At the start of that sentence, I was in solitary confinement, utterly alone.

I still claimed to myself that I was anti-Catholic. There was, however, unbeknown to me, a Catholic impulse within me. I despised communism and was disgusted by cynical consumerism. A few years earlier someone had suggested that I begin reading the distributist[2] writings of Chesterton and Belloc.[3] I was actually being drawn closer to Mother Church faster than I could have realized at the time.

During this second prison term, I read Tolkien's *The Lord of the Rings*, which gave me a sense of objective goodness and virtue. Then some well-meaning saint sent me some rosary beads. My father used to dismiss Catholics as "bead rattlers", so to me rosary beads were just artifacts of papist superstition and idolatry.

But here I was, utterly desolate. My suffering was intensified because I was becoming disillusioned with my politics, the one thing that had held my life together and given me some sense of meaning and purpose.

It's one thing to suffer heroically for one's cause; it's another type of suffering when you no longer buy into the cause. When I'd been sent to prison a few years earlier for the same charge, I was a fanatic, and I saw myself as a political prisoner. Then it was easy to remain defiant and hoist the banner. But by the second imprisonment, my cause had been undermined by my reading of Chesterton and Belloc. So here I was a so-called political prisoner who no longer sympathized with the politics for which he was a prisoner.

Al: That's got to create a huge vacuum in one's heart.

Joseph: Exactly. I had this vacuum of desolation on the one hand and these rosary beads on the other.

Now, I had no idea how to say the rosary. I didn't know the Hail Mary or the Glory Be or the Apostles' Creed. I had been taught the Our Father when I was a child, but I'd long since forgotten it. So I had no way of saying the rosary as it should be said. Nevertheless, I began to mumble and fumble, and for the first time in my life I prayed.

Al: Prison is not a bad place to lose one's spiritual virginity.

Joseph: And so it was in this moment of desolation and emptiness and suffering that I made my first efforts to communicate with our Lord. And all I can say is that answers came.

I made great progress very quickly. I started to go to Mass. One of my major steps on my path to Rome was beginning an active prayer life. And that prayer life began in what you just described as the vacuum of desolation.

Al: So you were willing to try something to see if God was really there?

Joseph: Exactly. I was an agnostic nonbeliever who was beginning to wonder whether perhaps God did exist. And I'd reached the stage, thanks to my reading of Chesterton and Newman and Belloc and others, where I thought, *if* God is really there, then probably the Catholic Church has it right. I didn't need converting to Catholicism from Protestantism.

By the way, I need to do justice to my late, greatly loved father. He was very anti-Catholic, and he had much to do with my spiritual deformation, I won't deny. I didn't inherit anti-Catholicism with my mother's milk, as it were, but with whatever fathers give.

Al: Mother's milk, father's sweat. How's that?

Joseph: I guess that will do. But I have to tell you that my father was received into the Catholic Church about ten years before his death, when he was in his sixties. And he died a very, very holy death. All he wanted to do the last two years of his life was pray the rosary, which I take as a miracle.

Al: With good reason. Many spiritual writers teach that the greatest miracle is the miracle of repentance and the conversion of a soul. Now, back to your conversion: How long were you in prison?

Joseph: I actually served six months of the twelve-month sentence; this was in early 1986. When I got out, the first thing I had to do was extricate myself from my political affiliations and all my comrades. That was difficult. Imagine being involved in a political movement from the age of fifteen, and now you're twenty-five.

Al: Plus you were no ordinary foot solider. You were a leader, an articulate political prisoner. You had served two prison terms for "the faith."

Joseph: Absolutely. I mean, these people thought I was a great hero. And I felt like a hypocrite and an imposter, because I no longer believed the sort of things that they believed. And so the difficulty was, how do I extricate myself?

The only thing I could do was physically remove myself from London and move out to the boondocks—or the English equivalent of the boondocks, in East Anglia—slowly pick up the pieces and start a new life. And so I continued my progress toward the Church.

Al: You needed to disengage, quite literally. In AA alcoholics are warned against "the geographic cure." But with your political attachments, this move seems perfectly sensible. It may not work with alcoholism, but it certainly works with bad relationships.

Joseph: It certainly does. And most of my relationships were bad, and this severing was absolutely necessary. And of course this brings us back to the initial thing that I said about "no pain, no gain." Some of these people were friends, in spite of the fact that we had differences now. And I had to sever those friendships.

Al: Did any of those friends eventually pick up on your story of conversion?

Joseph: Yes, it became a topic of conversation among them. Many treated it with contempt and considered me to be lost, a traitor to the cause, a believer in this Jewish nonsense and Christianity and so on. But I get two or three blasts from the past via the Internet every year: former colleagues contacting me to say that they also have become Catholics.

Al: Isn't that something? Now, is this principle of "no pain, no gain" a recurring principle for you?

Joseph: Absolutely. God has used the hardest moments in my life. Probably the most devastating moment in my life was when our daughter was stillborn.

Al: Yes, I remember that.

Joseph: I don't seem to be very articulate when talking about it. But what I can say is that I remember as it happened, looking up at the crucifix above our bed—the baby was stillborn in our home—and crying inconsolably. And feeling not peace—because I was in too much suffering to feel at peace—but at one in a mystical sense with Christ on the cross, in a way that I hadn't really felt before and haven't since. I understood as well as I've ever been able to the real suffering that he had to endure for us.

So this mystical union was only possible by actually being nailed to the cross in some way myself. And this continues to be a major thing for me: spiritual growth through suffering.

Al: Did you ever have a period, as a Christian, when you didn't believe in redemptive suffering?

Joseph: No, never. The Catholic view of suffering was with me from the beginning of my conversion.

I was born and baptized a member of the Church of England, but I was a Christian in name only for the census records. I was brought up essentially as an agnostic. And my conversion was really from agnosticism to Catholic Christianity. So I had all the anti-Catholic prejudices of a certain type of Protestant but none of the positive Protestant faith.

Al: And when were you finally received into the bosom of the Church?

Joseph: It was on the Feast of Saint Joseph, 1989. I'm still amazed.

ROBERT LOCKWOOD
Mass Disturbance

[It is called] Holy Mass (Missa), *because the liturgy in which the mystery of salvation is accomplished concludes with the sending forth* (missio) *of the faithful, so that they may fulfill God's will in their daily lives.*

—*CCC*, 1332

Robert P. Lockwood is director of communications for the archdiocese of Pittsburgh. For many years he was president and publisher of Our Sunday Visitor Publishing. He still writes his popular "Catholic Journal" column for *Our Sunday Visitor* and is a regular contributor to other Catholic publications. His *A Faith for Grown-Ups: A Midlife Conversation about What Really Matters* is a humorous reflection on growing up and growing old Catholic.

Bob: I love to show in my writing how grace builds on nature. We find it in a bus ride, in cooking soup or in an afternoon snowstorm. But when I look back on a *moment* of spirituality, a moment that truly made an enduring difference, I have to climb in the Way-Back Machine.[1]

And I land in December 1968, when I was a sophomore at Fairfield University. Actually I was a student revolutionary, as we all were in the sixties. I always liked that line, "What did you major in?" "I majored in the sixties."

Fairfield University was a fine Jesuit school when I was there, from 1967 to 1971. It was almost all male, almost all Catholic.

Mine had been the usual traditional Catholic upbringing. And somewhere around sophomore year in high school, I had taken the "last train for the coast." The nuns had taught us the tenet, "Act as if you have faith, and faith you will have." I did the opposite. I stopped practicing the faith and developed an atheist affectation.

I wasn't really an atheist. But I never went to Mass, never went to the sacraments, never did anything. It's a sociological curiosity: I don't recall any of the guys on my dorm floor, though we were all Catholic, who actually attended Mass. We even had a chapel in the basement of the dorm. All these kids were like me, brought up in a pretty traditional way, but miniskirts and rock-and-roll happened. It wasn't outright spiritual rejection as much as spiritual apathy. We had better things to do, or so we thought.

I went home for Christmas, back to the old home, the old neighborhood, the parish of my childhood, where I'd had the sacraments in school and gone to church prior to the Second Vatican Council. And that's when something special happened, though I didn't realize it was special at the time.

Now, my brother Toby was and is a bit of an odd duck. He's a brilliant linguist who taught himself three languages and was kind of a Latin scholar to boot, but he was an indifferent student at best. He would tend to slip in and out of various emotional and intellectual fads. One month he would be into Nostradamus, the next month obscure Russian novelists; you know the type?

That Christmas of 1968, Toby was going through what he would call later his "Catholic moment." OK? He had decided to return to the Church. He was about twenty-three years old.

Looking back, I think Toby's was kind of an "ashes and incense" reversion rather than a conversion. He experienced a kind of "smells and bells" attraction. Strangely, he was the only one of us who had been mostly educated in public schools. So I think he had a different perspective. The rest of us had had enough incense to clear out our sinuses for twenty years.

But that Christmas, 1968, Toby had his sights set on getting me to go to Christmas Mass with him. Now, I hadn't attended Mass since my sophomore year in high school. And again, I was living that atheist affectation.

By the way, I thank God that my mother isn't around to hear that. Because if she had known that I was skipping Mass routinely, whoa! But I had the whole thing down. I'd go somewhere, find somebody who had gone to Mass, make sure I knew what the sermon was about...

Al: Come home with the bulletin...

Bob: Yeah, yeah. All that stuff I had down pat.

I think I was discovered the summer after my freshman year in college. I had been out all night and was trying to sneak into the house at six o'clock on a Sunday morning. My father had gotten up to walk the dog. I was walking in the door, he was walking out, and he looked at me and said, "I suppose you're not returning from early Mass."

Al: Hardly.

Bob: So it was December 23, and Toby and I decided, as brothers did back in those days, to stay up late drinking beer—copious amounts, as I recall—and we got into one of those great philosophical and theological arguments. I was taking this very materialistic position, while my brother was arguing from his recently rediscovered Catholicism. At one point, after I had posited something particularly foolish, my brother said, "Are we just slabs of meat that talk?" And something about that line hit me.

I paused, because the one thing I knew for sure was that *I* wasn't a slab of meat that talked. I knew in my essence that I was more than that. And so it was a line that somehow managed to slip through the foam and fog of the beer and make some sense. Toby then—being the wise debater—said (right at that point, because he knew he had me a little bit), "Rob, make me a deal. Just go to Mass with me on Christmas Day."

And I said, "Uhhhhh,...uhhhhh,...I'll go to Mass on Christmas Day." I figured, what was there to lose? There was a certain nostalgic element.

On Christmas Day we walked to 10:30 Mass, at my old parish of Christ the King. It was one of those balmy Christmases with just a remnant of a previous snowstorm. Being Yonkers, New York, what snow remained was now black. We walked past some of the old haunts.

I had spent eight years of grammar school going to that parish church. We walked into church, and I turned right away to the boys' section. Of course, there was no "boys' section" at 10:30 Mass on Christmas Day, but I could no sooner sit on the other side of the church than abandon who I was.

I knelt down and looked around, noting that next to nothing had changed since the place had last seen my shadow four or five years before. But just the physical features of the place touched me. I remember looking at the Stations that I had seen, oh, a hundred million times when I was in grammar school. Here they were, the same Stations of the Cross. Even their physical presence meant something to me.

The organ and the choir started with some Christmas carols, which got me a little bit nostalgic, maybe even a little hopeful that something was going to be different. But now here comes what I call my two-part punch line to this long story, OK? Part one, *I got absolutely nothing out of that Mass.*

Al: Nothing, and you were emotionally primed for it?

Bob: No fear and trembling, no life-changing homily, no sudden spiritual insight. After the Mass my brother asked me what I thought, and I said, "Meaningless," and I meant it. And we headed home.

But here's part two of the punch line: *I came back to the faith on a full-time basis about two years after college.*

Can you drift back to the faith, just as you drift away? To a certain extent that's what I did. But here's the deal: That "meaningless" Christmas Mass was my moment of grace. It started an itch in me, and I trace my return to the faith to that Mass.

Al: That "meaningless" Mass?

Bob: That "meaningless" Mass, halfway into which I was examining the ceiling and then trying to find something in the pew that I could read to distract myself. Not a day goes by even now that I don't think of that Mass, because it ended up being so pivotal in my life. There was no immediacy to it, no "right now." It wasn't like Saul of Tarsus and his blinding flash on the road. I didn't come running out, I didn't speak in tongues, I didn't do anything.

But there was an astounding moment of personal grace for me. Despite all the fits and starts, despite all the idiocy that I would continue to do in my college years, my thinking had changed. Something had started. At some point in that Christmas Mass—how can I put it?—I was open to the grace of God, and I let it in without knowing it.

Al: How did it work its way out?

Bob: *How* it worked its way out is another story. My conversations were never the same after that Mass. During the pseudointellectual arguments that I had on campus, I slowly started becoming a defender of faith, if not even *the* faith. Eventually I started *really* studying theology in the required theology courses and not just putting in the work. I started reading books, none of them great intellectual things but simple things like *Your God Is Too Small* by J.B. Phillips[2]—wonderful little book. And these things started to pile up on me.

It takes a long time to beat apathy. How I finally secured my return was through a vow I made during one Lent to attend Mass every day. And that sealed it. But I really don't consider *that* my reversion to the faith. I really consider my reversion to the faith Christmas Mass 1968, 10:30 AM at my old parish in Yonkers, New York.

So my critical moment of grace I attribute to the Mass, a brother and too many beers.

WILLIAM DONOHUE
Caught By Catholicism

> *The right to the exercise of freedom, especially in religious and moral matters, is an inalienable requirement of the dignity of man. But the exercise of freedom does not entail the putative right to say or do anything.*
>
> —*CCC*, 1747

Willliam A. Donohue began his teaching career in the 1970s, working at St. Lucy's School in Spanish Harlem. In 1980 Bill was awarded his PH.D. in sociology from New York University.

Bill is the author of many articles and three books: *The Politics of the American Civil Liberties Union, The New Freedom: Individualism and Collectivism in the Social Lives of Americans* and *Twilight of Liberty: The Legacy of the ACLU.* He is currently working on a book titled *Secular Sabotage: How Secularists Sabotaged America.*

He is currently the president of the Catholic League for Religious and Civil Rights, the nation's largest Catholic civil rights organization. The publisher of the Catholic League journal, *Catalyst,* Bill is also an adjunct scholar at the Heritage Foundation, and he serves on the board of directors of the National Association of Scholars.

The occupational hazard of a watchdog is the tendency toward ill temper, perpetual grievance and self-righteousness. Bill has been given the grace to avoid these pitfalls. He is a man of valor, unafraid to fight the good fight, but his wit, tenacity and keen eye for hypocrisy are borne along by a fundamental magnanimity of spirit. Not only has he amply defended the Catholic Church against individual bigots and anti-Catholicism, which often lies beneath the veneer of many of our cultural institutions, but only God knows the number of personal conversions that Bill's tough but judicious style of confrontation and resolution has made possible.

Bill: Here's a story that I'm delighted to share. When it happened I didn't realize just how momentous it would be in my life.

After going to Catholic schools, I wound up in the Air Force during the Vietnam War. The Air Force trained me as an accountant.

Like a lot of young men, I was partying with the boys, and I got lax. I never really questioned my faith, but I only went to Mass occasionally. I was just too caught up in that whole cycle of hanging out with the guys, going to the pubs and things of that nature.

When I turned twenty-three, I left the service. I decided to work full-time while I finished my master's and pursued my PH.D. at New York University. I had been working part-time as an athletic coach in a Catholic school, and I really did enjoy the kids. Even though I had been offered some nice-paying accounting jobs here in New York City, that wasn't in my heart. I really wanted to do something that I felt called to do. And I thought I'd like to be a teacher.

However, there was a problem: I had never taken a single education course in my life, so I couldn't teach in the public schools. I thought, well, the Catholic schools don't have the same criteria; maybe I can get a job there.

I wasn't astute enough to think maybe I should go to the archdiocesan department of education. Had I done so, I would have found that they had a waiting list a mile long at that time, back in the seventies. Instead I literally picked up the phone book, turned to "Schools" and scribbled the addresses of fifty-nine "Saints" in Manhattan, the Bronx and Queens. I applied to them all.

Al: No!

Bill: Yup. I only heard from one. Even the people in the archdiocese's bank of prospective teachers didn't want to go there. It was in Spanish Harlem, a rough neighborhood. That didn't bother me: I'm a big guy. And beyond that, I was studying for my master's in sociology, so I had a tremendous interest in people—ethnicity and religion and whatnot.

I started teaching the third grade, but the next year I was teaching seventh- and eighth-grade social studies and religion. Here's a guy who had been pretty lax in the Air Force and had gotten just a little bit better after that. But the principal forced me to teach religion.

Now, I couldn't—unless I was going to be a hypocrite—teach religion with the same verve with which I taught social studies if I wasn't "into it." I needed to bone up on a few things. So I read more and started going to Church more. And one thing I noticed was that I was teaching religion using textbooks that were void of anything spiritual.

Al: I think by common consent the 1970s were not one of the Church's strongest catechetical moments.

Bill: It was almost impossible. Everything was dumbed down. We had a picture of a bearded Jesus-looking guy sitting in a garbage can with a peace sign. It was all "love your neighbor." The textbook gave so little content that all it contained were empty platitudes.

In 1975 my school principal asked me to attend a meeting of the religion teachers in the elementary and secondary schools in the archdiocese. It was a jam-packed meeting, with a hundred people or so—

almost all nuns and priests and a couple brothers. I may have been the only layperson.

The moderator of the meeting asked if we teachers had any questions. I stood up and said: "Can you tell me, how am I supposed to teach religion using a religion book that doesn't have any religion in it?"

Well, I was a bit green—I was a young man—and I had no idea that there was this turmoil going on in the Church. Remember, the last time I had been into anything in religion was at the cusp of things changing. The Catholic Church had changed so quickly and not for the better in many respects.

That dumbing down had shocked me, but what really shocked me was the reaction to my question. The room exploded. Half the people were for me, the other ones, well, I think they wanted to kill me.

Al: Bill, you had the ability to polarize people from the beginning, even when you didn't know it.

Bill: I am a polarizing figure today, and sometimes I do that intentionally. But this was all by accident. I just couldn't believe the reaction.

I said, "Listen, given how empty these religion texts are, our kids could make the slide from being a Catholic in high school to being an atheist in college very quickly. There's nothing to hold on to here. If you look at the first three commandments, obviously they mention God, but what about four through ten? Any atheist can accept 'treat your neighbor well' and that kind of thing. There's no grounding in Christ and in our Blessed Mother."

I set up a firestorm. Next thing, guess who gets elected chairman of the religious education council for the archdiocese of New York?

Al: I'll guess that was you.

Bill: Right. Now, this threw a positive burden on me. I felt, wow, I can't believe I got myself into this thing. And this was occurring just as I began to gravitate back to my religion.

I believe this was an expression of Divine Providence. This was no accident. I wasn't sure why it was happening, but I felt I had to go with the trajectory, with the vector of change. And that vector moved me closer to the Catholic Church.

This turned out to be a defining moment, because I've never left the faith since. A number of years later, I was teaching at a Catholic college, and then I became, in 1993, the president of the Catholic League.

Al: That is amazing. I love the hidden hand of God in all these things.

Bill: That's just it. Now I can see that God called me, but I didn't really know it at the time.

When we look back on our lives, certain things begin to make sense. Even some of the things that we're not too happy about start to look like pieces of the puzzle, and they form a pattern. This was a defining piece of the puzzle in my life.

Al: From the beginning your calling put you in a place of public responsibility.

Bill: It's not as if I sought it out. The Lord just pulled me along on this trajectory, which landed me years later at the Catholic League for Religious and Civil Rights.

When I was at the Heritage Foundation, writing the book about liberty *(The New Freedom: Individualism and Collectivism in the Social Lives of Americans),* somebody said to me, "Bill, your idea about freedom really fits in with what Fulton Sheen[1] was saying." I said, "What?" This stuff had become part of my thinking, even when I didn't realize it.

Of course, the encyclical *Veritatis Splendor* by Pope John Paul II is the most extraordinary document on morality, liberty and the necessity of having individual responsibility and not just rights as the requisites for a free society. It just blows away John Stuart Mill's 1859 essay "On Liberty."[2]

Al: When it comes to the meaning of freedom and truth there is a very large chasm between John Paul II and John Stuart Mill.[3]

Bill: In Mill you can do whatever you want as long as you don't harm somebody. On the one hand that sounds fantastic. But then try to craft a society on that principle. How do you determine harm?

As I looked at my own writings, I noticed that my intellectual interest had always focused on liberty in society. I began to see the good fit between the Church's teaching on liberty and what was good for society. The Church's teachings *did* have an effect on me even when I wasn't consciously aware that I was coming from a Catholic orientation.

Now I look back and get a kick out of that, and I'm very proud of it because I can see how the work connects to God. It's been an incredible experience for me.

FIVE

Faith Under Fire

•

•

•

•

•

•

JERRY USHER
God Is Big Enough

The fidelity of the baptized is a primordial condition for the proclamation of the Gospel and for the Church's mission in the world. In order that the message of salvation can show the power of its truth and radiance before men, it must be authenticated by the witness of the life of Christians.

—*CCC*, 2044

Jerry Usher is the host of *Catholic Answers Live* and program director of Catholic Answers Radio. He has nearly thirty years of professional radio experience, creating and hosting many programs over his career. He had a hand in starting the Immaculate Heart Radio Network in 1996. Few people have been so dedicated to the service of the gospel through the medium of Catholic radio. Jerry is one of the Catholic radio world's true pioneers and spokesmen.

Jerry received a bachelor's degree in theology and philosophy from Franciscan University of Steubenville and went on to graduate studies, spending six years in formation for the priesthood from 1989 to 1995. Continuing his interest in vocational discernment, he coedited *Called by Name: The Inspiring Stories of 12 Men Who Became Catholic Priests.*

Jerry: My story begins toward the tail end of my seminary formation, in the summer of 1995. I was completing a unit of clinical pastoral education in the Twin Cities. My brother and his new wife lived in that area, and I thought it would be fun to spend the summer with them.

A hospital in the Twin Cities accepted my internship, and I was assigned to an oncology ward—not an easy assignment, as you can imagine. I saw a lot of people die and found myself in many challenging pastoral situations. It was tough but rewarding work.

A cancer patient I'll call Mark celebrated his twenty-first birthday in the hospital. Mark really didn't trust anyone. I found out later that he came from a background of drinking, drugs and heavy metal music.

None of the hospital chaplains were able to connect with Mark, so I guess they were glad when someone younger came along. They assumed that I would have more in common with Mark. So they said, "Jerry, we'll give you a shot at him."

At first Mark was cold and unreceptive. "Lord," I thought, "you're going to have to do something here." I felt called to persist, so as a matter of routine, I would sit at the foot of his hospital bed and pray the rosary. Sometimes he would pretend to be asleep, which I thought was kind of cute. He was very shy and very insecure.

Al: So you would actually sit on his bed, praying the rosary while he pretended to be sleeping.

Jerry: Yeah. He knew I was there. He was completely conscious and lucid. He just didn't want conversation.

After a while Mark began to open up. We'd have short conversations, and eventually I'd ask him questions like, "What do you think happens after this life?" and, "Have you ever thought about God?" He would share what little he had to say. He obviously had had no formation in religious and spiritual things.

Al: Was he hostile when you raised spiritual questions?

Jerry: Not really, because by this time he had learned to trust me. He saw that I appreciated him for who he was and that I wasn't after anything.

Al: You weren't forcing any issues.

Jerry: I wasn't trying to convert him. He knew that I just wanted to be there. He was a human being, and I guess I showed love for him by those acts of simply being with him.

Al: I call it "the ministry of presence."

Jerry: It wasn't a matter of going in and saying, "Mark, do you want to talk about God? No? Good. I'll be leaving now." He saw that I cared about him as a person.

For instance, he really didn't get many chances to get outside the four walls of his hospital room because of the treatments and his failing health. Eventually, however, I got permission to wheel him outside.

When it became clear that he wasn't going to leave the hospital, that he was going to die, Mark got very angry. Apparently the doctors had initially given him reasons for hope. Things were looking good for a while, but then, all of a sudden, the doctors said, "You know, Mark, there is nothing we can do for you."

When he was near death, Mark was moved to the hospice wing. I began to pray for an opportunity to present the gospel and get him baptized. And this is the reason I wanted to share this particular story with you. The most enduring lesson for me was that God is big enough to do things outside the box. Sometimes we simply have to let go and let God be God, not bound by our expectations.

I was sweating to get this kid baptized. I talked with the hospital chaplain. I talked with the Catholic priest. I talked with Mark's parents, who said, "We are not very spiritual or religious, but OK, we'll let you do that."

So everybody was on board, and we had this window of opportunity. So I scrambled to find the chaplain to get this thing done now. But by the time Father Foley got back, Mark's parents had second thoughts. I just said, "Ohhhh."

It was then I learned the lesson: "Lord, I have to let this go. There's got to be a way you can save Mark, even without baptism."

My plans had been thwarted, but I didn't walk out on Mark. One afternoon I was sitting in his room and a family friend, who was also a Christian, dropped by. We began talking about how we might help Mark spiritually. Just at that moment his respiratory therapist walked in and said, "Hey, Mark, time for your treatment." Mark had been unresponsive, but when he heard his therapist call his name, he sort of bounced up, very groggily—his head was just bobbing around—and received a brief respiratory treatment. All of a sudden I looked at this family friend and said, "This could be Mark's opportunity."

I had talked to Mark previously about the importance and effects of baptism. So I seized this moment and asked, "Mark, do you remember when I talked to you about baptism?"

He was kind of nodding his head yes, but he was signaling something like, "Tell me again. What is it?"

So I again shared the good news of God's grace through Christ and how baptism unites us with Christ in his death and resurrection. Then I felt emboldened to say, "Mark, I'd like to offer you the opportunity to be baptized."

I kept glancing over at the family friend to make sure that she agreed that Mark was responding of his own volition. He asked me a few questions, and I said, "Mark, I want to be perfectly clear that you don't have to do this, but it is something I'd like to make available to you." And Mark consented.

So I opened my Bible to Matthew 28:19, dipped my fingers into a little cup of water that was on his nightstand and traced the Sign of the Cross on his forehead, saying, "I baptize you in the name of the Father and of the Son and of the Holy Spirit." This had to be the quickest baptism in Church history.

Mark lapsed back into unconsciousness, and I breathed a sigh of relief. Beautifully the biblical text goes on, "Lo, I am with you always until the close of the age," reassuring Mark (and me) of Christ's ongoing presence.

I asked the hospital staff to keep me in the loop as Mark approached death. One evening my brother and I were out playing basketball when my beeper signaled that the end was near. I ran home. I don't think I even took a shower. All the way to the hospital I prayed, "Lord, please let him hang on. Let him hang on. Let him hang on."

Mark died five minutes after I entered his room. But to be with him and his family at that moment profoundly moved me. Afterward two family members, independent of one another, told me that Mark had obviously waited for me to be there for his final moments on earth.

Al: What a privilege. Did you see the family again?

Jerry: Yes. At his wake I learned more about Mark. The family displayed a stack of his concert ticket stubs about three inches high. I studied the pictures of him in his leather jacket and long hair, posing with alcoholic beverages and drug paraphernalia. It drove home to me how his life choices had not predisposed him to yearn for baptism. All I could think was, "Lord, you are so awesome."

Al: If I can indulge myself with a play on words (Saint Paul gives me permission to do so in Ephesians 5:18: "Do not get drunk [controlled] with wine…but be filled [controlled] with the Spirit."), you had been operating under the influence of God's Spirit and, by God's grace, had the privilege of midwifing Mark into the kingdom of God.

Jerry: So now I feel that I have a saint in heaven praying for me. I've asked for his intercession many times, and I'm sure he's praying for his family, who did not realize that he had been baptized and had become, hopefully, a saint that day.

Al: Ah, Jerry, I love that. I love the way that you were faithful without being aggressive. You weren't discouraged by this young man's initial resistance. You respected his freedom and the significance of his choice. Obviously he had come to trust you. Many of those outside Christ are like Mark and don't even want to ask questions until they feel as though they are dealing with a sound, faithful person.

Jerry: Yes. He never would have trusted my understanding of the faith and accepted baptism at my hands had it not been for those long afternoons at the foot of his bed and taking him out in his wheelchair and other basic caregiving. I look back now and realize I made some right decisions in spite of myself.

Al: Yes. It's always consoling to remember that the Holy Spirit is working ahead of us, even before we begin sharing Christ.

Jerry: Right.

Al: Jerry, thank you for strengthening us, for building us up in the faith, by sharing your most enduring spiritual lesson.

Jerry: Thank you for the opportunity. I've shared Mark's story with friends before but never this publicly, and I'm very happy to do so because it shows the greatness of our God. He is bigger than we can imagine.

TIM STAPLES
Seized By Grace

The way of perfection passes by way of the Cross. There is no holiness without renunciation and spiritual battle. Spiritual progress entails the ascesis and mortification that gradually lead to living in the peace and joy of the Beatitudes.

—*CCC*, 2015

Tim Staples fell away from the Southern Baptist faith of his childhood and came back to faith in Christ through the witness of Christian televangelists. After a four-year tour in the Marines, he enrolled in Jimmy Swaggart Bible College and became a youth minister in an Assembly of God community. During his final year in the Marines, however, Tim met a Marine who challenged him to study Catholicism from Catholic and historical sources. Tim was determined to prove Catholicism wrong, but he ended up studying his way to the Catholic Church in 1988. The story is told in Patrick Madrid's *Surprised by Truth*.

Tim spent the following six years in formation for the priesthood, earning a degree in philosophy from St. Charles Borromeo Seminary in Overbrook, Pennsylvania. He then studied theology on a graduate level at Mount St. Mary's Seminary in Emmitsburg, Maryland, for two years. Tim left the seminary in 1994 and has been working in Catholic apologetics and evangelization ever since.

Tim is the author of *Nuts and Bolts: A Practical Guide for Explaining and Defending the Catholic Faith.*

Tim: I was fresh out of the seminary in 1994, and St. Joseph Communications in California hired me to do Catholic apologetics. I was excited about traveling and speaking; I was in heaven.

Out of the blue I began to have seizures. They started as *petit mals.* I had a couple of seizures even during talks. I would just lose it; I couldn't speak anymore. The first couple were a few months apart, and then they began to grow in intensity and frequency. Al, I had seven *grand mal* seizures in one day.

Al: I can't imagine trying to take the podium with the fear of that in mind.

Tim: It looked as if my career as an apologist was over. I would lose track of my thoughts, and I couldn't remember Scripture.

It seemed as though everything was collapsing around me. I was ready to move back east and try to start over.

Al: Did you have any idea what the cause of the seizures was?

Tim: No, and that was the hardest part: the uncertainty. For two years I had neurologists and doctors doing everything—doing EEGs, EKGs, CAT scans, the whole bit—and they could not find what was causing the problem.

They were pumping me full of drugs, continually increasing the dosages. I was sluggish and could hardly think anymore. I was at the end of my rope. In my heart I knew God was calling me to apologetics, but I just couldn't do it.

As I was getting ready to head back east to do only God knows what, my boss, Terry Barber, founder and director of St. Joseph Communications, called me into his office and said, "Tim, we're going to take you out of the HMO, and we're going to find out what's going on with you. I believe God has called you to be an apologist."

Terry told me that he was going to send me to specialists and pay for it himself.

I tell you, Al, I erupted in tears. I could not believe what I was hearing. Here was true Christian charity in action.

I saw several specialists, and they found the cause. I had three surgeries, and I've been completely healed since 1999.

But you know, Al, through the whole thing—which lasted two and a half, almost three years—I learned a lot of things. One was that my faith was not very strong. It's one thing to run around and preach at folks, but I tell you, when it happened to me, I wasn't real pleased with the way I responded. I found myself falling at times into despair.

I discovered that I'm not real good at reaching out for help. I would go to my spiritual director, and at other times I would *run* from my spiritual director. Overall I would give myself an *F* on my spiritual report card.

But I did see the grace of God at work in Terry Barber, in friends and in my wife, Valerie, who was my fiancée at the time. She went through this whole thing with me. She had friends and even family members—and God bless them, they had her best interests at heart—who told her, "Look, you've got to break up with this guy. You don't know, you could have a vegetable on your hands here."

Al: "Get out while you can, before it gets worse."

Tim: Exactly. And I'm not bitter toward any of them, because I understand where they were coming from.

But Valerie spent several nights sitting with me in hospitals. She saw the seizures. My roommates would call Val, and she would come out with her twin, who was a nurse. So she wasn't blind to what I was going through, and it was excruciating for her. But when people told her to break this thing off, she said no. She knew that she loved me.

And I'll tell you, waking up in a hospital and seeing her asleep in a chair next to me, I was overwhelmed with her love. Our love was really formed in the crucible there, and when I came out on the other side, I could see how God purified me in so many ways. He humbled me and really helped me appreciate the gifts that I have in my life.

Al: Is that because you felt them stripped away from you?

Tim: Exactly. And I really didn't know if I was going to have my fiancée leave me as well. You know, there was uncertainty there.

Al: And you're a tough guy. You spent four years in the Marine Corps: That tends to toughen a person up.

Tim: You know, I like to think I'm the tough guy, a former boxer and Marine and everything else, but I found myself completely humbled and shredded, and I really believe the Lord put me back together. And all I can say is that God's grace and mercy are the only reason I'm here. God picked me up out of the depths, as the psalmist says (see Psalm 18:16), and healed me. He healed me physically, but he healed me spiritually in ways I don't even yet understand but will learn as I go.

Al: Do you feel that—for lack of a better term—this "baptism" in suffering that you went through was also related to effectiveness in future ministry?

Tim: I have to believe that. There's a danger of turning the faith into an argument. The faith can become a stack of books rather than an intimate relationship with our heavenly Father, through our Lord and Savior Jesus Christ, mediated through the graces that come through the Church and other members of the body of Christ. Some converts come into the Church and isolate themselves. There's an intellectual pride that leads to all sorts of craziness. Al, you've seen this as well as I have.

God knew exactly what I needed. Those years of suffering made me a much better person and a much better Catholic.

SIX

Family Ties

•

•

•

•

•

•

JENNIFER ROBACK MORSE

He Does as He Wills

*If God is almighty "in heaven and on earth," it is because he
made them. Nothing is impossible with God, who disposes his
works according to his will. He is the Lord of the universe,
whose order he established and which remains wholly subject
to him and at his disposal.*
　　—*CCC*, 269; Genesis 49:24; Isaiah 1:34; Psalm 24:8–10; 135:6;
　　　　　　　　　see Jeremiah 27:5; 32:17; Luke 1:37

Born into a Catholic working-class family, Jennifer
Roback Morse earned a doctorate in economics during her twelve-
year lapse from the faith. A committed career woman before having
children, she taught economics for fifteen years at Yale University
and George Mason University.

Doctor Morse's scholarly articles have appeared widely, in *The
University of Chicago Law Review, Harvard Journal of Law and
Public Policy* and elsewhere. More popular articles and columns have
appeared in *Forbes, The Wall Street Journal* and *National Catholic
Register*.

Doctor Morse is founder and president of Ruth Institute, an educational institute that promotes marriage as a fundamental gender-
based social institution. She is the author of *Love and Economics:*

Why the Laissez-Faire Family Doesn't Work and *Smart Sex: Finding Life-Long Love in a Hook-Up World*.

Jennifer: My most enduring spiritual moment or lesson surrounds my infertility.

Like many people, I left the Catholic faith during my college and early adulthood years. I earned a doctorate, married, divorced and then remarried. Once I had tenure my husband and I thought, "Now it's time to start having kids."

My plan was that I would get pregnant during the summer, birth in the spring and put my baby in day care in the fall so I could go back to work. That's what most of my women colleagues had done. I was in control. I had it all planned.

Imagine my surprise when the baby didn't arrive during the month that I had set aside for that. I became very upset, as women so often do when they face infertility.

Al: How long before you knew you were dealing with an infertility problem and not just a timing problem?

Jennifer: I thought something was wrong instantly, but my husband said, "Come on. Calm down, please." The infertility specialists don't even want to talk to couples until they have been trying to conceive for a year, because within a year 85 percent of people like us will conceive. Then it went on for four and a half years, so that counted as a problem.

Every month I was getting more upset about it. And as time went on, it became clear that, whether the problem was resolved or not, I wasn't getting my way on my schedule. And that was very upsetting to me. It was in that period of time that I found myself drawn back to the Catholic faith.

Al: Why? What was the appeal?

Jennifer: Well, it's hard to explain in natural terms, Al. I think the Calvinists would call it "irresistible grace": God hits you over the head with a two-by-four, and you start to shape up. It would have been possible for me to resist, although I don't see how I could have.

Between my home and my office there was a church. On my way to work, I would stop for 6:30 AM Mass. It was a catacomblike experience: a very elderly priest saying Mass for a handful of businesspeople. And I would be at the back of the church, with tears streaming down my face at the consecration, thinking to myself, "I don't believe any of this. What am I doing here? What is this all about?"

After Mass I would find myself in front of the statue of the Virgin Mary. As time went on it started to become clear to me what was going on: At a time like this a girl wants her mother. And my mother was far away and not available for a variety of reasons, so there I was with Mary, the Mother of God.

I began to allow myself to think that I was not in charge of all outcomes. My whole adult life had been premised on the claim that I *was* in charge of everything. Infertility gave the lie to that boast. That's what made infertility a deeply spiritual experience.

So I started to come back to the faith. This involved getting an annulment of my first marriage[1] and asking my husband if he would go through the regularization of our marriage. But in his mind this had nothing to do with him. So I did the whole annulment process with the help of a wonderful priest at George Mason University.[2]

Looking back on it, graced elements kept appearing. One of my dearest colleagues, unbeknown to me, was a practicing Catholic. Leonard Liggio[3] was at the Institute for Humane Studies while I was at the Public Choice Center in the economics department at George Mason. We were very close, free-market libertarian friends. Leonard gently paved the way for me to see that commitment to the Catholic faith was an intellectually respectable thing. I had swallowed the idea that church was for losers and for people who didn't think for themselves—blah, blah, blah and all that kind of stuff that sounds so foolish now.

Leonard was really a great man. He was trained at Georgetown in the old days when Georgetown was staffed by men of vast learning and great wisdom and intellect—you know, the whole Jesuit training.

Al: When Jesuits were giants, I think, as Father Cornelius Buckley has written.[4]

Jennifer: That is how Leonard felt about them: They were intellectual giants. And so, all of a sudden, I felt, "I can still be an intellectual and be Catholic—wow, that's really cool." It's funny now to think about it, but that is what I thought.

Al: Many people don't realize it, but the Catholic tradition teaches that natural reason can discover the existence of God and, in some way, actually participates in the eternal Word, the *Logos*, you might say, the "logic" of God.

Jennifer: Absolutely. But I didn't know any of that. What the heck. I knew economics; I didn't know any of this other stuff.

Leonard also introduced me to the campus minister, Father Bob Cilinski, who had created a vibrant Catholic presence at George Mason. He was the priest who saw me through the annulment process. After that my current marriage needed to be convalidated.

My husband was reluctant. He felt that I had done a bait and switch on him. But he held his nose and went through with it.

We had our marriage convalidated at St. Louis Catholic Church in Alexandria, Virginia. Father Cilinski witnessed it, along with a handful of friends. The morning of the ceremony, my husband said to me, "You know, I'm kind of nervous," which I thought was very sweet. It was a way of renewing our commitment to one another.

But through all this we still didn't have any kids. I was learning, however, to let go of the outcome. As we went through various kinds of infertility diagnostics and so on, I became less and less stressed about it.

It turned out that my next-door neighbor once had an infertility crisis, and she sent me to her infertility specialist who, as it turned out, worked at a Catholic hospital—Providence Hospital in northeast Washington, D.C. So again by the grace of God, I was working with infertility people who were operating within the Catholic tradition. By the time we were done with all the diagnostics, I was ready to listen to what the Church had to say about what you could do and not do with regard to infertility.[5] I knew that the Church knew some things that I didn't know.

Another grace was that long before our infertility experience, my husband used to like to watch these nature/technology TV programs. We watched presentations of these innovative methods of in vitro fertilization and GIFT and all those things. He would be saying, "Wow, isn't that cool?" And I would be thinking, "Isn't that disgusting? I'm never doing that; I don't care what happens. I'm not donating my body to science while I'm still in it."

What's interesting to me is the revulsion that I felt, even when I was not being a Catholic. I often have thought that it was the grace of the sacraments—the indelible sacraments—still protecting me, the grace of my baptism and confirmation.

And that was a huge protection, Al, because we joined an infertility support group, and I'm telling you, some of those women were crazed. They were willing to do anything. We saw people go through their savings, use up all their insurance benefits, practically bankrupt the household going through treatment after treatment after treatment. I am so grateful that I was able to put the brakes on all that.

While the women were hysterical, the men were helpless. They were trying to make their wives happy, but they couldn't make them happy because the one thing the women wanted was not really in their husbands' power to give.

Al: Rachel weeping for her lost children, or in this case inconceivable children, could not be consoled (see Matthew 2:18).

Jennifer: My husband and I started seeing how different men and women are.[6] A therapist told us that men and women respond to the infertility experience very differently. We weren't prepared for that. We were all about equality, sameness and all that stuff. But knowing the differences between male and female is a darn good thing to have in your mind before the boys and girls arrive.

The most enduring, the most important spiritual lesson that I learned was that we are not in control of all the outcomes. It's the beginning of humility to know that God is God and you're not. It allows you to allow God to be God, and then you can be human, and then your spouse can be human. And I think that the infertility experience was very good preparation for parenthood, because if you think that you're in charge of all the outcomes, when children arrive on your doorstep, you are in for a rude shock.

Al: It's incredible to watch God redeem a situation that we reluctantly have given over to him. I see that you are a mother and a foster mother. How did that all happen?

Jennifer: Well, in 1991 we had finally let go of having kids naturally, and we applied to adopt a child from Romania. The adoption agency called in January. They said, "We've got a little boy for you; what do you say? He'll be two years old." We said, "Great."

Ten days later I went to the doctor with a head cold and found out I was pregnant. So that's how God gave us our two kids.

Then, from 2003 to 2006, we were foster parents for San Diego County. We "had" eight children, usually two at a time, just by answering the phone. That's a lot easier than infertility treatments!

RAY GUARENDI
Divine Adoption

God reveals his fatherly omnipotence by the way he takes care
of our needs; by the filial adoption that he gives us. ("I will be
a father to you, and you shall be my sons and daughters, says
the Lord Almighty.")
—*CCC*, 270, quoting 2 Corinthians 6:18; see Matthew 6:32

Doctor Ray Guarendi is the father of ten, a clinical psychologist, author, public speaker and, arguably, Catholic radio's most engaging and humorous host. I first interviewed Ray nearly twenty years ago when his second book, *Back to the Family*, was published and he was making the talk show rounds to promote it. When I received a review copy of the book, I noticed that it wasn't written for an explicitly Christian audience. As a psychologist, he clearly understood the importance of "faith" in holding a family together. The nature of that faith, however, was left an open question in the book. During the interview, we both spoke in general terms about "faith" and its "utility."

Though we didn't discuss it, we were both reconsidering our relationship to the Catholic Church. Six or so years later, we met again as Ray was finishing a speech at a nearby public school. He had a trunkful of *Surprised by Truth* and other works of Catholic apologetics that he was handing out. At that time I had just begun forming Ave Maria Radio: It was a spiritually delightful reacquaintance. A few months later we were both hosting programs for a national Catholic radio network. We've been friends as well as colleagues since.

Doctor Ray's radio shows *The Doctor Is In* and *On Call With Dr. Ray and Friends* can be heard weekdays. He has been a regular guest on national radio and television, including *Oprah, The 700 Club* and *CBS This Morning.* He has written several books, including *Discipline That Lasts a Lifetime: The Best Gift You Can Give Your Kids, You're a Better Parent Than You Think!: A Guide to Common-Sense Parenting*—now in its twenty-fifth printing—and his newest book, *Good Discipline, Great Teens.* Ray's work also involves school districts, Head Start programs, mental health centers, substance abuse programs, inpatient psychiatric centers, juvenile courts and a private practice.

Doctor Ray: My urologist told me, "If you have children, I want you to go on the afternoon talk shows, because it will be a miracle. Doctor Ray, you are not equipped to have children."

I had something they called Sertoli cell-only syndrome, present from birth. (My grandmother was pleased that at least it's Italian.) I couldn't have kids: zero, nada, not a one.

My wife, Randi, and I said, "We sure would love to have a large family, but we're not going to have one now." You can't adopt six kids; maybe we'd get one or two.

My wife was coming into her Christianity. She said, after prayer, "Let's send out letters to attorneys and see if they will pick our name." So we wrote eight hundred letters to attorneys. They sat in the corner. My wife's mother came over and said, "Randi, send those letters out."

Within a day or two, we got a call from an attorney who had a seventeen-year-old girl in his office, right off the street, wanting to release her baby for adoption. Now, this attorney was seventy years old and had never done an adoption. When the girl came to him, he said, in essence, "I got some letter in the mail yesterday. I was getting ready to pitch it." So he pulled out our letter.

When Andrew was born we were ecstatic. Unfortunately he had a cleft lip and palate, but we figured that made it less likely that the birth mom would reconsider.

OK, we got our kid. I guessed that was it in the adoption game. If you get one, maybe two, you're lucky. But we stayed on a list at an agency, and one day we got a call. "We have a little girl for you."

Al: Really? How did that happen?

Doctor Ray: They told us, "Well, the birth mother said she always wanted a big brother growing up, and she never had one. And you are the only people on the list with a little boy."

So now we had a boy and a girl. End of story: American family. That was it. But we told the agency, "By the way, if you ever come across a child you might have difficulty placing, call us."

A year later I received a call at work. A little biracial girl was born. Surprise. "Would you be willing to adopt her?" Of course! We had hit the lotto. Wow, three! End of story, right?

At my fifteen-year class reunion, I started talking to a woman who had adopted black children. I didn't know you could do that. She gave me the name of an attorney in Columbus, Ohio. We contacted the attorney and told her we were open.

Lo and behold, the birth mother of another biracial baby saw our name and said, "Oh, there's a biracial sibling. And this guy's a shrink. If my kid has any problems, I'd rather he be with a shrink."

OK, so we had four. That's enough. Right?

Al: I assume that at this time you were solidly committed to Christ?

Doctor Ray: Yes, but I was skeptical. People were saying, "This is God's hand!" I was saying, "Hmmm, maybe it is, maybe it isn't."

Al: What was Randi saying?

Doctor Ray: She was saying it was God's doing. She can see these things better than I can. I didn't want to attribute anything to God that maybe he just allowed to happen.

But it gets better. I was sitting there after a talk that I gave, and an adoption worker looked at me and said, "You're Italian, aren't you?"

I said, "*Sì.*"

She said, "I have two little kids who need to be adopted, and they are part Italian and part Hispanic. They look just like you!"

So I went home to my wife and said, "Some lady has these two kids who need parents."

And Randi said, "Ray, we have four little kids." At that time they were all five and under. The kids waiting to be adopted were both four years old.

So I said, "Why don't we just apply?" OK.

We were not picked as the first family. The first family went to meet the children, and the children were so bratty that the family dropped out. The second family got divorced. We were the family of last resort. So the call came: "We have two children for you." All right. Six kids, all six and under. End of story. Done.

Meanwhile, my wife was going to eucharistic adoration, even though she was not yet Catholic. She said to God during adoration, "We're done, God. If you want us to have another kid, you're going to have to just drop that child in our lap."

The next day we received a call from the attorney in Columbus. "I have a baby boy who was supposed to die in the womb." The young mother had been told a blood clot growing next to the baby would kill him, so she didn't have to "do anything." Well, the baby was born two months premature: three pounds, intensive care.

The attorney said, "The only other family I have is in Washington State. Are you interested?"

My wife, of course, had just said to God, "You have to drop that child in our lap." What are you going to say to God, "Never mind. We're done"?

So we went and saw this little guy, all wired up and with tubes everywhere. He looked like a ferret. Peter is ten years old now. Al, from the time he was old enough to talk, he has not stopped talking about wanting to be a priest.

We have adopted three more children since. The birth mom of our last child, Elizabeth, went to the abortion clinic in her seventh month. Of course, you know what an abortion in the seventh month is like: It rips the child apart. The girl screamed when she realized that and ran out of there. She called us the next day.

We were not expecting a tenth child, Al. It was an unplanned adoption. We weren't practicing safe phone.

Al: You can't be too careful!

Doctor Ray: I believe the hand of God, at every step along the way, revealed itself clearly with each of our children. I could offer the same types of "coincidences," if you will, for others of our children.

Al: Coincidences are God's futile efforts to remain anonymous.

Doctor Ray: Well put. Even a skeptic like me had to admit that maybe God was pulling a few strings.

Back when we got the news that we were not going to be able to conceive, I was thirty-five, and my wife was thirty. Doing the math, Al, even if at that point we had no fertility problems, what do you figure would be the number of kids we could have, max? Four or five maybe?

Al: Sally and I started having children when I was thirty and she was twenty-six. We had four children. Then there was a nine-year gap, and we had David. So over twenty years we had five.

Doctor Ray: So you can figure it would be like that for us, five or six max. The irony is—and this is where I see God's gentle mercy—we were saying, "There goes our dream for a big family. Close it up. Shut it down." And he said, "I'll give you ten."

Al: This is one of the great operational principles of the Christian life: We die to a vision; we die to a grand idea; we die to ourselves; and God lifts us up and blesses us beyond all expectations. Some of us are in the blessing phase, and others are still dying to a vision, awaiting the resurrection of it.

Doctor Ray: You know what the danger is? There's so much pride in us. Even with the gift of children, one of his greatest gifts, we have to watch that we don't feel like, "Something must be pretty good about us to get that gift. He must have thought we were pretty special." Intellectually we say, "No, that's his unmerited favor." But that pride is so deep inside that its alien, ugly head is always lurking around.

I view it this way: God is not going to say to a famous basketball player, "Hey, come on in. I've always watched you. I've always wanted you up here in heaven." He doesn't choose any of us that way. God didn't choose the Hebrews because they were a mighty nation or great in population (see Deuteronomy 7:6–11).

Saint Paul tells the Corinthians:

> Not many of you were wise by human standards, not many were powerful, not many were of noble birth. But God chose what is foolish in the world to shame the wise; God chose what is weak in the world to shame the strong; God chose what is low and despised in the world…so that no one might boast in the presence of God…. As it is written, "Let the one who boasts, boast in the Lord." (1 Corinthians 1:26–30, 31, *NRSV*)

DOUG KECK

His Grace Is Sufficient

[E]ven the most intense prayers do not always obtain the heal-
ing of all illnesses. Thus St. Paul must learn from the Lord
that "my grace is sufficient for you, for my power is made per-
fect in weakness."

—*CCC*, 1508, quoting 2 Corinthians 12:9

Doug Keck is senior vice president for programming and production at EWTN, the world's largest religious media outlet. For twenty years Doug headed up TV operations at the media conglomerate responsible for Bravo, AMC and the Playboy Channel. He was called to EWTN, working very closely with Mother Angelica. He was given the responsibility for transforming the on-air look and program quality of EWTN radio and television.

Doug: I was raised in a "mixed family." My mother was Catholic, and my father was Lutheran. I spent some time in public school and some time in Catholic school.

My dad was good about going to Mass, but I certainly didn't grow up in a vibrant Catholic environment. It was a decent Catholic upbringing but certainly not one that was engrossed with participation in parish activities or a daily rosary. There was not a lot of sacred art in our house.

Al: What did you want to do as a kid?

Doug: I wanted to play center field for the New York Yankees. That's what every boy in my neighborhood wanted to do, unless he wanted to play center field for the New York Mets.

Later I worked in New York sports. I had the great pleasure of knowing Mickey Mantle. I was his liaison for one season, when he was announcing for our sports channel.

Al: Where were you at that point spiritually? What were your priorities?

Doug: I had the same goals that I think a lot of people have: I was planning on leading a decent life, but I wanted to be successful and make money. After wanting to play for the Yankees, I worked in cable television for a number of years. I worked on the start-ups of some movie channels—Bravo, American Classics. I even worked for a period of time on the Playboy Channel.

Not that my wife and my family didn't mean anything to me—not at all. But television and media are beasts that never rest. Even the Catholic media needs to be fed, but there is a higher level of stress in the secular environment, where so much money is at stake. If you don't perform you're out.

Al: With hardly a word either. You can come in and do a broadcast on a Friday afternoon and never return.

So you wanted to be successful, but it wasn't a success at any cost. Your family was important to you.

Doug: Yes. I married my high school sweetheart. We had gone out for a few years after high school, throughout college, and then married. We were doing well.

The only issue we had was difficulty having children. For me at the time, it wasn't that important. I thought, children are nice, but they're also a financial obligation. To my wife it was much more important.

Al: Were you worshiping together?

Doug: Certainly. However, I was quite open to Sister Mary Feelgood's advice that if you didn't get anything out of Mass, you didn't have to go. I think that's partly because I grew up in a household with a Lutheran father and a Catholic mother. My mother was sick later in her life and couldn't always ensure that we were getting to Mass.

My wife knew better: She had some guilt about missing Mass. Her family was all Catholic and had been involved in the Church. She was invested in living the faith consistently.

Al: How did you deal with your trouble starting a family?

Doug: It was tough. I reconciled it to myself by simply recognizing that I loved my wife, and if it was just going to be the two of us, so be it. But having children was something my wife felt very strongly about, and she wanted to take additional measures to make that happen.

Eventually we did have two children, a son, Matthew, and a daughter, Caitlyn. My son was born under stress, but only later did it become evident that he was autistic.

Al: When did you begin to suspect that he might have autism?

Doug: I tended to pooh-pooh the symptoms my wife noticed. He was born with his eyes crossed, which we honestly didn't realize until later. He underwent multiple surgeries; that certainly indicated something wasn't right.

But it was when we watched him with other kids that we noticed, "Wow, he's behind." When you're dealing with just one child, through the eyes of love, you don't see these things. But when there's a benchmark, it is easier to gauge the development of a child.

Initially we thought Matt was in an ADD type of situation. Only later, when we finally went to a doctor, did we realize that his case was more severe.

Al: What kind of spiritual stress did this put on your understanding of God's purposes?

Doug: I was lucky, in a way, that I didn't really understand what Matthew was going through until after I had had a spiritual reawakening. The Lord spared my going through that without some sort of spiritual underpinnings. I don't know how I could have done it without faith to uphold me. The way this happened demonstrates the goodness of God.

When Matthew was four years old, a doctor told us that he was autistic. It was a Friday, and that weekend my wife and I were part of a Marriage Encounter team giving a retreat weekend.[1] In that way the Lord distracted us. He gave us a chance to take in the news and to take it in as a couple, working together with two other couples, a priest and the Holy Spirit. God lovingly cradled us for that weekend.

Al: That's about as perfect an environment as I can imagine for coming to grips with this new challenge to your faith and family. On the one hand, as a presenting couple you were there to share with others. But a Marriage Encounter weekend also encourages personal transparency and introspection and grasping what you're dealing with as a couple.

Doug: That's right. The format and routine that encompass a Marriage Encounter weekend helped us come to grips with what this really meant. It's not that Matthew would be just a little hyperactive and in a few years calm down. No, this was a lifelong situation that would impact his life and ours until death did us part.

Al: Once the Marriage Encounter weekend was over, how did you and your wife handle this challenge?

Doug: Part of the challenge was coming to grips with exactly what this diagnosis meant. My wife was concerned mainly with how it impacted longevity. Did this mean Matthew would not have a full, long life? We were happy to find out that autism has nothing to do with lifespan.

Then it was a question of what could we do to maximize his abilities? How could we help him lead the fullest life possible? We focused on going forward.

Al: What obstacles did you run into?

Doug: We're going back about sixteen years here. In the last five to ten years, autism has become much better understood. Also the varying degrees of functionality are better understood.

Back then we were still dealing with things like the "refrigerator mother" syndrome. This was a theory that autism was caused by mothers who had not attached properly to their children. It came from a flawed study years before. For years mothers with autistic children were being blamed because they hadn't loved their children enough. We were lucky that that was beginning to become passé, but it was still lingering.[2]

Another challenge was the nature of autism. It's not like diabetes: We basically know what causes diabetes and what you're supposed to do if you have it. With autism there's a spectrum of different issues, and the kids are not all the same. So how do you treat these children when they're all different? You have to sort out what's right for your child. Matthew, fortunately, is a very high-functioning autistic.

There were multiple enduring lessons that came out of this challenge. One, from Marriage Encounter, is that marriage takes three. You have to put God at the center of your marriage.

Another lesson was that God's grace is sufficient.[3] That's something I can attest to, in moving from New York to Birmingham, Alabama, among other things. The Lord has always supplied the grace that was needed for us to get through day by day—not more than what was needed but just what was needed.[4]

Another lesson is very simple, and I can see it from having worked in the secular media and at EWTN. That lesson is, you have to put your trust in God and not in the world, because God will never let you down (and the world always does).

TIM DRAKE
A Double Portion

*The marriage covenant, by which a man and a woman form
with each other an intimate communion of life and love, has
been founded and endowed with its own special laws by the
Creator. By its very nature it is ordered to the good of the couple, as well as to the generation and education of children.*

—*CCC*, 1660

Tim Drake began as a scrivener at age six, and he has been
stringing sentences together ever since. He has published more than
six hundred articles, in *National Catholic Register, Our Sunday
Visitor, Faith and Family* magazine, *Catholic World Report*,
CatholicExchange.com, *Columbia* magazine, *Gilbert!* magazine, *This
Rock* magazine and many other publications. He serves as senior
writer with the *National Catholic Register* and *Faith and Family* and
is the author of *Behind* Bella*: The Amazing Stories of* Bella *and the
Lives It's Changed* as well as editor of *There We Stood, Here We Stand:
Eleven Lutherans Rediscover Their Catholic Roots.* He and his wife,
Mary, and their children live in St. Joseph, Minnesota.

Tim: I appreciate the invitation to share publicly this story of God's providence in the midst of loss and suffering.

About three years into our marriage, Mary and I decided it was time to have children. But God did not bless us with children. This became a very difficult struggle.

I was working as a teacher and Mary as a sign-language interpreter at a university in the Twin Cities. I was Lutheran, and she was Catholic. Each Sunday we would worship at both the Catholic and Lutheran churches.

Finally, in August of 1994, we conceived. It had been a long time in coming, and we rode all of the emotions that accompany a long-awaited pregnancy. We called our family members and our friends, sharing the news with them, and then settled into the exciting process of waiting.

Al: I sense something ominous about to happen.

Tim: I came home after a day of work. Mary was upstairs, and I was downstairs near the banister. I can still picture the scene and hear her tone of voice. "Tim, could you come upstairs?" I knew something wasn't right.

Al: Lord, have mercy.

Tim: I found Mary in the bathroom. She had begun bleeding. We called the nurse and then the doctor. We didn't know what was happening.

"Certainly it could be a miscarriage," our doctor explained. But he couldn't tell for certain, and he suggested that we wait the night and see what happened. The night passed with difficulty—praying, crying, not knowing. The uncertainty tormented us.

Al: How far along was Mary in the pregnancy?

Tim: Approaching two months. And sure enough, it was a miscarriage. Our first child was dead.

Even in this day and age, a generation after the revolution in women's health and medicine, miscarriage is not something that many people are at ease discussing. And for us it was difficult, first of all in the loss of our baby, but then we had to call all those people whom we had heralded with the news of our blessed event. That's when it became clear to me that people, understandably, aren't really comfortable responding to the loss of a child.

Al: But respond we must, so how did people respond?

Tim: One person made light of it, saying, "Well, you know the fun part is trying." Others said, "You're young. You can have more." Others were more sensitive. They would just quietly say, "Oh, I'm sorry to hear that," and send a note or a card. One exceptional response came from a couple whom we didn't even know very well: They planted a tree in honor of our child.

But through it all there was this sense of loneliness. We tried to fill the void with each other. We spent a great deal of time together grieving and realizing that Christ also suffered alone.

We focused on embracing the cross, realizing that whatever kind of suffering we endure, we ultimately do it alone, at least in the temporal sense.

Oh, should I mention that we also tried to compensate for our loss by getting a cat?

All of this, Al, coincided with my drawing nearer to the Church. It was probably within a month or so that we ended up naming the child Gabriel (the angel of the Annunciation to Mary) and I started looking into the Catholic Church by attending an RCIA class.

Al: Did you read some kind of providential significance into the coinciding of those events?

Tim: I'm sure that there is some supernatural significance there. Then on March 19 of 1995, the Feast of Saint Joseph, the husband of

Mary, I was received into the Catholic Church. Wonderfully enough, about the same time we were also blessed to conceive again.

It struck us as truly remarkable that—given our personal circumstances—my Mary's pregnancy would coincide with the months of the Blessed Virgin's pregnancy. And it was a wonderful pregnancy. Mary delivered Elias Joseph two days after Christmas 1995.

Al: Glory to God in the heavens, and peace to his people on earth.

Tim: We were consoled in our loneliness after the miscarriage by remembering that Jesus suffered alone. Then we saw God encouraging us through his providential control of circumstances. But there was another lesson for us. The lesson was that in loss is gain. The paradox of Christian spirituality is that in weakness is strength and in death is life. While we had lost Gabriel, we had gained Elias.

Al: L'Arche is a Catholic community where persons with severe developmental disabilities live with those who can assist them in work and prayer. The story is frequently told of how John Paul II embraced one of the more disabled and said, "In your suffering fulfill your vocation." He didn't say, "Suffering is your vocation," but, "In your suffering fulfill your vocation." Every one of us is called to be conformed to the image of Christ.

It looks, Tim, as if you and Mary were identifying yourselves with Christ and the Holy Family, you were fulfilling your vocation, and your suffering was made fruitful rather than fruitless.

Tim: Yes.

Let me bring the story to a close in much the same way that I began it. Two years after Elias was born, we conceived again. Just as in the first pregnancy, everything seemed fine Then Mary went out shopping one day with her mother and came home bleeding. Again we called the nurse, and again she suggested waiting. (I don't know why they do that, but we waited the night to see what would develop.) We were scheduled for an ultrasound the next morning. It seemed like a virtual repeat of our first go-round.

Elaine, my wife's mother, came with us the next morning, as did Elias. We all piled into the exam room to watch the ultrasound images. The technician knew our history and was respectfully taking her time with the pictures. Finally she turned to us and said, "Your baby is fine...*both of them*." And thus we learned that we would be having twins.

Mary had been bleeding this time because the babies were growing so quickly. We went in expecting the worst and came out doubly blessed!

JEFF CAVINS
Redeem the Time

The divine fatherhood is the source of human fatherhood....
Parents must regard their children as children of God *and*
respect them as human persons. *Showing themselves obedient*
to the will of the Father in heaven, they educate their children
to fulfill God's law.

—*CCC,* 2214, 2222; see Ephesians 3:14

In *My Life on the Rock* Jeff Cavins tells the story of his return to the Catholic Church after twelve years as a Protestant pastor. Jeff founded and hosted EWTN's *Life on the Rock*. With Matt Pinto he created the Amazing Grace series of books. But Jeff is perhaps best known as the creator and principal author of the *Great Adventure Bible Timeline* learning system, which he presents in seminar form throughout the English-speaking world.

Jeff is also currently the director of the Archbishop Harry J. Flynn Catechetical Institute in the archdiocese of St. Paul and Minneapolis. He and his wife, Emily, reside in Minnesota with their three daughters, Carly, Jacqueline and Antonia.

Jeff and I hosted morning and afternoon drive-time radio programs respectively during 2003–2004. Through our colaboring as brothers in Christ, I witnessed his extraordinary love for the Word of God understood in the tradition of the Church, coupled with a Christlike transparency and commitment to principle that is rare. As well as anyone I've met, Jeff lives what he teaches.

Jeff: One of the most enduring spiritual lessons for me took place back in 2003 when Emily and I dropped off our firstborn daughter, Carly, at Franciscan University in Steubenville. I was not prepared for the emotional and spiritual impact that leaving my firstborn daughter a thousand miles from home would have on me.

Al: You're an intelligent, future-oriented father. You certainly knew that one day she would go off to college.

Jeff: I did, but to start with, Al, we struggled to have Carly. Emily and I were married back in 1978 and struggled with infertility for eight years. I told God: "If you'll just give us a child, I'll do the best job possible. You'll never be disappointed in me, Lord, in how we raise our child." And then he blessed us with Carly.

We have always made an effort to teach her the Scriptures, to pray and to serve the Lord. But we fell into a routine pattern of life, thinking we had years and years ahead of us to raise our kids. Then before I knew it, high school graduation hit me.

We've always been attentive to Proverbs 22:6, "Train up a child in the way he should go, / and when he is old he will not depart from it," and Ephesians 6:4, "Fathers, ... bring [your children] up in the discipline and instruction of the Lord." But the month before Carly left, I started paying more attention to her. I started to notice her beauty, her face and how much she looked like my wife. I wanted to spend more time with her: "Let's go have a cup of coffee." "Let's talk."

And then it was the day of departure. The van was packed with all of her belongings, and I started to choke up.

Al: Did she notice your sense of loss?

Jeff: She started to get a little bit weepy, and so did my wife. All five of us got in the car. (Our two beautiful adopted girls were four and six at that time.) As we were ready to back out of the garage, it hit me: Life would never be the same again. I said, "Excuse me. I forgot something." Even as I talk about it now, I get emotional.

I went back in and went downstairs to Carly's room. I stood in the door and looked at the bed all nicely made up. I picked up her pillow and smelled it. I looked at her childhood books and thought again to myself, "Life in the Cavins household will never be the same."

I gathered myself and went back upstairs. My wife said, "What did you forget?" and I said, "Oh I just forgot some things." We got in the car and started driving.

Al: How long a drive was it?

Jeff: It took two days for us to get to Steubenville, and all the way there I kept looking in the rearview mirror. That was kind of a metaphor for life as a father. The Lord was telling me, "Don't always be looking in the rearview mirror. You have two more children at home. Look forward, and take the opportunity to be with your kids and to teach them and to love them and to wrestle with them, whatever it might be."

When we got to Steubenville, I thought to myself, "This is great; we've got four days of orientation, four days left with Carly." But pretty soon that was over. And that's one of the lessons I've learned in this whole business of raising children and dropping them off at college: Time flies, and that final day will come, sooner or later.

I told Father Michael Scanlan[1] that I was really struggling with letting go of my daughter. And during the final orientation meeting, I went outside and wrote a five-page letter to Carly, which rehearsed all that I'd been through with her as a father, what I had tried to teach her, how important people were and how important was her choice of a husband or religious vocation. It was really a love letter from a father to a daughter.

Finally it was three in the afternoon, time to say good-bye. At Franciscan University there's a big cross on a hill. I went over to Carly, and I said, "Sweetheart, will you walk over to the cross with me and Mom and the girls?"

She asked, "Why?"

I said, "You'll see."

We walked up to that thirty-foot cross. I looked at Carly and said, "Sweetie, this is where I want to leave you, at the foot of the cross. This is what we've been pointing to our whole lives. This is the place of change. This is the place you go when you have trouble. This is the place you look to when you struggle with anxiety. And remember that Jesus Christ loves you, and he has a plan for your life."

We had a custom in our house: Every morning I would lay my hands on my daughters' heads and pray the Aaronic blessing: "The LORD bless you and keep you: / The LORD make his face to shine upon you, and be gracious to you: / The LORD lift up his countenance upon you, and give you peace" (Numbers 6:22–27).[2] I said, "I want to pray for you this last time."

I placed my hands on her head, but that wasn't good enough. I put my arms around her and prayed for her and told her how much I loved her. It was a very emotional moment for the whole family.

We got in the car, and we started to drive away. You could see in her face that she was struggling. That was how we parted.

On the way home, for the first two hours my wife and I didn't even look at each other. We just kept our faces straight, tears constantly streaming down our cheeks. Two hours after we left, the cell phone rang. It was Carly.

Al: Did she need money already?

Jeff: Funny, Al. No, it wasn't that. It was simply, "Dad, I miss you." I said, "I miss you too."

Al: Even for those of us who enjoy parenting, even if our stewardship seems to be turning out well, there remains a bittersweet taste.

Jeff: Yes, because there is this necessary separation, and it is inevitably painful. But there is another bittersweet element.

You're a father, Al, and I'm a father. Everything in our spiritual and social DNA is crying out, "Take care of your little girl. Watch over her. Protect her. Don't let the bullies get her. Teach her what guys are like. And be with her when she needs you." And here I dropped her off. I drove away from her. I was doing the opposite of everything I know as a father.

Al: Leaving her at a moment of vulnerability.

Jeff: You said it well.

Al: What was it like when you got home?

Jeff: That first night we all knelt down to pray, which we normally do, and all of a sudden it hit us that one of us was gone. My wife and I started to cry a little bit.

My then-six-year-old daughter Jackie said, "What's wrong?"

I said, "Well, Carly's not living here anymore, and it takes some time to get over things like this."

And Jackie said, "I'm over it." And I remembered the Lord's word about the rearview mirror.

I'm reminded of Ephesians 5:16: "[Make] the most of the time, because the days are evil.... Understand what the will of the Lord is."

So dropping off my daughter at college, with two daughters still at home, was a life lesson. I learned that time flies by, and I need to grab that time and make the most of every opportunity. I'll never have yesterday again in my life, but I do have today and tomorrow. The good news is that the Lord can redeem the time. It's never too late.

SEVEN

What You Win Them With
Is What You Win Them To

•

•

•

•

•

•

FATHER FRANK PAVONE
Rescue Those Being Led to Slaughter

Since it must be treated from conception as a person, the embryo must be defended in its integrity...like any other human being.

—*CCC*, 2274

Father Frank Pavone was ordained a priest for the archdiocese of New York by Cardinal John O'Connor. He is president of Priests for Life and the author of *Ending Abortion: Not Just Fighting It!* He is seen daily on EWTN and heard on Vatican Radio.

Father Frank was with Terri Schiavo in her final moments. Blessed Mother Teresa asked him to address the clergy of India, and the Vatican asked him to help coordinate pro-life activities throughout the world.

Father Frank also serves as president of the National Pro-life Religious Council and pastoral director and chairman of the board of Rachel's Vineyard, an international retreat program for postabortion healing. In 2004 he established a community of priests permanently dedicated to full-time pro-life work. He serves as the first moderator general of the Missionaries of the Gospel of Life.

Father Frank: I want to share with you what really galvanized me to the point of saying an iron door was closed behind me.

While I was a parish priest at St. Charles on Staten Island, New York, I heard that there was going to be a Rescue at an abortion clinic.[1] The exciting thing was that we didn't know which clinic it was going to be.

I invited a few of my parishioners to come with me and rescue some babies. "We don't know what's going to happen, but who's willing and ready to come with me?" A few brave parishioners decided to come. My pastor said, "I need you back to say the weekend Mass. Don't get thrown in jail."

We had to get up at three in the morning and go to the home of a local Staten Island activist. I'll never forget walking in there. People were arriving, embracing each other. Things were really quiet and dark. There was kind of a hushed anticipation of the rigors of the day.

I sat down at the dining room table, and the activist's wife came over to him and said, "Here are your Rescue glasses." He changed his glasses because he didn't want the good ones to get damaged.

We got into a car, and we were given a little card that told us to go to a shopping center. There some people gave us another card. This happened about three more times until we eventually found ourselves at an abortion facility in Levittown, New York. People converged on this place and blocked the doorways, putting themselves between the babies and the instruments of death.

I was moved beyond description. I stood there praying and counseling women who were delayed getting in because the place was blockaded.

As the morning unfolded, police arrived, helicopters flew overhead, and eventually buses arrived to cart off those getting arrested. The police warned people to get away from the door. A spokesperson for the people said, "We cannot get up and walk away from this door, because if we do, we are allowing these children to go to the instruments of death. We will not move."

Al: Rescuers make visible the unborn who are slated for death. By risking arrest they say to the world, "Take us in the place of the unborn." To the unborn they say, "Those who reject you reject me."

Father Frank: Precisely. We are quiet, and we don't give our names, just as the babies are quiet, and they don't even have names yet.

As the morning went on, I saw many people carried away, including priests I knew. I looked into the windows of one bus and raised my hand in a blessing. Many people on that bus had peaceful smiles on their faces. They had been through a rigorous morning, sitting out there for seven or eight hours with nothing to eat, nothing to drink and now facing arrest. They were filled with the joy of the Spirit. It was beautiful.

Al: Many people have told me that this act of identifying with the unborn child was a watershed moment for them. Others have told me that it was a particularly clarifying moment because they saw the forces of light and the forces of darkness clearly drawn.

I participated in a dozen or so Rescues myself. We were middle-class, law-abiding citizens and largely churchgoers. We were not your sixties-style rebels.

To find ourselves arrested was a shock.

Father Frank: Yes, very shocking, absurd really. That is what stirred my soul that day. This was not abstract; this was not theological. Here was the culture of death right in front of us. Good people were being dragged away, and babies were being dragged to death.

I stood there and said, this has got to stop. I committed myself that day to making this the goal of my life.

The parishioners who were with me experienced the same kind of thing. I was with one of them later that evening at a birthday party. Everyone was talking, laughing and greeting one another. We were sitting there with these people, but it was as if we were in a different world. We looked at each other and said, are you feeling what I am feeling? We had been taken into this deeper awareness that there is a holocaust going on around us and we've got to stop it.

Al: Would Priests for Life have come into existence without that experience?

Father Frank: Yes, I believe so. Right around the same time some priests in California decided they wanted to encourage their brother priests to preach the pro-life message. That was the actual beginning, the first seeds of Priests for Life. I joined then, and two years later I became the first full-time director.

I had been on this path from my high school days. In 1976 I went to the March for Life in Washington and was stirred. But after my participation in Rescue, I literally felt that I could not go on with life's business without devoting my ministry completely to ending abortion. Now that has given rise not only to the expansion of Priests for Life but to this new society of young men who are committing themselves to full-time pro-life work as an expression of their priesthood.

Al: Do you remember Bishop Austin Vaughan?

Father Frank: Oh, yes. I remember his story of one of his most enduring moments. He looked at his ring and realized that the three people engraved on it—Jesus, Peter and Paul—had all been arrested and thrown into jail for standing up for what was right. He saw this Rescue stuff going on, and he said, "Wait a minute, what is holding me back? Fear of jail? Then why am I wearing this ring?" He became, as you know, a marvelous sign, example, teacher and leader nationwide.

Al: With your participation in Rescue, a door shut behind you. If this door hadn't shut, what might have been Father Pavone's future?

Father Frank: I've always been interested in academic advancement. I would very likely have inclined toward further studies as a priest and maybe teaching in seminaries. I very much wanted to do that in the area of biblical studies in particular. So, had the diocese agreed, I might have gone to the *Biblicum* in Rome and come back to teach at Dunwoodie in New York. That was one trajectory I could have followed.

But that door had closed behind me, and I came to a point of integration. My mental and physical energies had been going in several different directions. I was doing some teaching. I was doing parish work and pro-life work. I had my personal interests and studies. But after my encounter with Rescue, all that energy and all that desire to do good focused on the issue of abortion. I said yes, this is big enough to consume my whole life.

There was no turning back. I saw too much and too closely what was happening to these babies and women. I knew I could never walk away and say, "Well, yeah, I know they are killing babies, but I am going to do something else." I had come to a point from which there was no return.

REGIS MARTIN
A Man of Fiery Being

*The world, and man, attest that they contain within them-
selves neither their first principle nor their final end, but
rather that they participate in Being itself, which alone is
without origin or end.*

—*CCC*, 34

octor Regis Martin is professor of theology at Franciscan
University. He received his STD from the Pontifical University of St.
Thomas (the *Angelicum*) in Rome. He has written widely for the
Catholic press, including *Communio, National Catholic Register* and
St. Anthony Messenger, and has also contributed a number of pieces
over the years to *National Review*, a journal of secular opinion. His
books include *The Last Things: Death, Judgment, Hell, and Heaven,
Garlands of Grace: An Anthology of Great Christian Poetry,
Unmasking the Devil: Dramas of Sin and Redemption in the World of
Flannery O'Connor, What Is the Church? Confessions of a Cradle
Catholic* and, most recently, *The Suffering of Love: Christ's Descent
Into the Hell of Human Hopelessness.*

Regis and his wife, Roseanne, live in Wintersville, Ohio, with their
ten children.

Regis: Well, my moment of grace wasn't a conversion experience, and it wasn't, strictly speaking, even spiritual. It was an existential encounter that proved wonderfully fruitful and electrifying. It was when I first met Fritz Wilhelmson.[1]

This was way back in the summer of 1970. I was a callow undergraduate and found myself strangely catapulted to Catholic Spain, where beneath this immense poem in stone, the *Escorial*,[2] I sat at the feet of Fritz Wilhelmson, who introduced me to the science of being.

Al: The metaphysics of existence?

Regis: Yes, and it was unforgettable. It changed my life. It was a sea change certainly in my thinking, and I found my vocation as a teacher.

Fritz had this baroque exuberance about him, and he was dynamic and dramatic in the classroom. He was able to impart, in a particularly dazzling way, the importance of being. All of his classes were about being, about God; and this confrontation with "being" yielded rich insight.

For Fritz existence itself was understood in a wonderfully Chestertonian way: that it's good to be, because the alternative, nonbeing, doesn't have anything to commend it.

Al: I'll say!

Regis: God's name *is* Being. For Fritz the decisive text was Exodus 3:14, where Moses encounters God in the burning bush and inquires as to his name. "You're going to send me down with these tablets in stone. They're going to want to know who authorized this. What is your name?"

God thunders forth, "I AM WHO I AM." That became the great text for Saint Thomas when he explored the mystery of being: There is an *is*, as the common doctor would exclaim. For Fritz this became the pivotal moment in all of Western philosophy, and he was able to infuse that insight with great passion. This awakened in me a sense of wonder.

I once put together a collection of poems, *Garlands of Grace,* which I dedicated to Fritz. I said that he was the man who introduced me to the poetry of the transcendent. He was the finest teacher I ever knew. But for Fritz, I don't know that my life would have taken the shape and the form that it has, and so I am eternally grateful.

Al: How is it that some people have this sense of wonder at being, at the fact that some things are rather than are not?

Regis: It's the prime intuition. Fritz would tell us that it was at age ten, when he was on a bicycle going around a lake in Detroit, that metaphysical lightning struck him, and he was just amazed to find that he existed. This was a source of wonderment; this was miraculous.

Chesterton, I think, has the sense of it when he says (and I am paraphrasing here), "At the back of our brains there is this forgotten blaze or burst of astonishment at our own existence. I am and yet I need not be. There is nothing in me that can possibly account for my existence, and so it moves me to astonishment, it brings me to my knees, and it makes gratitude really the first obligation of sensate man."

Al: That's the first religious impulse, the realization that there is someone to thank.

Regis: That's right. If all life is a gift, then there is someone who is the Giver. This induces gratitude: I can never give sufficient thanks for the fact that God has made me. There is no necessity for me, and yet I am. This ought to be a cause of wonderment and gratitude; this is what makes people happy.

Chesterton speaks of the blasphemy of pessimism, and I think in his own life he sort of flirted with nihilism[3] but overcame it. In his autobiography, the chapter in which he explores this negation of life he calls "How to Be a Lunatic."

Nihilism is a kind of mental illness, and Fritz was wonderfully sane, just astoundingly healthy about the goodness of existence.

Al: So these issues moved you as a young adult?

Regis: Yes. I was a very young man, fresh out of college, this incredibly naively American student who had never left Pittsburgh and suddenly was in Catholic Spain, where this amazing theatrical personality was speaking to me in the accents of the universal doctor. His arguments for the existence of God crystallized for me that summer.

Al: Of the classical theist arguments, which did you find most persuasive?

Regis: Particularly the argument from contingency.[4] I remember Fritz's telling us that even Karl Marx was persuaded by that argument, but Marx went on to say that this was a question forbidden to socialist man, that man had to exercise a kind of willful repression. This was a cry of the heart, and yet it had to be somehow snuffed out, suffocated. No wonder socialism is pathological.

Al: Yes, that is why Soviet-style communism died: It had a bad anthropology. It did not understand that man had aspirations for something beyond this world.

Regis: Yes, the longing of the human heart.

You know, some years ago, at the university where I teach, there was a debate between Josef Seifert,[5] who is the great architect of phenomenology, and this ancient Jesuit by the name of Father Norris Clarke,[6] who is a Thomist. Seifert was going on and on at quite tedious length about the character of Cordelia in Shakespeare's *King Lear*—about the admirable virtues she embodied—when suddenly Father Clark interrupted and said, "Well, look, Josef, outside this window there is something even more extraordinary. There is a rock, and that this rock should exist is more thrilling, more amazing than this imaginary character from Shakespeare's play!"

That is the intuition into being that became the theme of Saint Thomas, of realism: that things are. Phenomenology is good, but it is interested in something less interesting: what things are; but that they should exist at all is a tribute to the largess of God. It was Fritz who awakened in me that sense of God's generosity.

Al: When you have moments like that, in what way do you relate them to the work of the Holy Spirit or to the work of grace?

Regis: Well, I think I experience an anointing from on high, from the Holy Spirit. For me this was an encounter with grace: the grace of this man who taught me a way of thinking, a way of being that would not only fulfill me, not only provide gainful employment but be a way of loving God, a way of serving God. I have worked at infusing others with something of this same enthusiasm that fired Fritz's soul. I have been at it now for twenty-five some years, and I am no end of grateful to him.

Al: And still full of wonder?

Regis: Oh, yes, yes. A childlike wonder, I think, is what we all need to cultivate. Saint Thomas, in his commentary on Aristotle's *Metaphysics*, says, "The reason why the philosopher may be likened to the poet is this: Both are concerned with the marvelous."[7]

Faith, Reason and Christopher Dawson

> *"The Church...believes that the key, the center, and the purpose of the whole of man's history is to be found in its Lord and Master."*
> —*CCC*, 450; quoting *Gaudium et Spes*, 10 §3; see 45 §2; *CCC*, 668

Professor James Gaston is founding director of the "Humanities and Catholic Culture" major at the Franciscan University of Steubenville, where he teaches all the integration of Humanities and Catholic Culture courses, courses entitled Catholic Political Thought and Comparative Politics and courses in history and geography. He is president of the Society of Christian Culture and editor of its publication, *The Dawson Newsletter*.

James: Al, thank you for the opportunity to think back on my life. I came up with three things that build on each other and can be distinguished but not separated. They are part of my intellectual and spiritual odyssey. I think these three points dovetail well, perhaps too well, with the unfortunate condition of the modern world.

I was raised in a small town in New York State. Growing up I had all of the best things, including Catholic schooling. And yet I got caught in the struggles of modernity.[1]

I was on my way to college, getting out in the world, in the early 1970s, and was going through some very intensive self-reflection. With the hindsight of a middle-aged academic, it would be fair to say that I was probably bordering on despair.[2]

Al: How did you keep from crossing that border, so that despair remained a moment rather than a way of life?

James: I ended up talking. I tried to find anybody who could help me out of my confusion over all the changes that were going on in society. I owe a debt of gratitude to a girl who belonged to a community of Christians that gathered at a barn on some farmland. It was called the Love Inn.[3]

Al: Yes. I've talked to other "alumni," like Phil Keaggy.[4]

James: Well, I talked with these people, along with my local Catholic priest and others, trying to make sense out of my life. I was in the dumps, further down than I'd wish upon anybody. I had a conversation one night with this girl, who kind of threw up her arms in her own little despair over me.

On the car ride home, I gave myself completely to God, and I begged him to enter into my life and save me. I don't know how to say it other than that he came to me in a car ride, somewhere between Ithaca and Courtland, New York, in 1971, and saved me.

Al: What did that teach you?

James: That God is palpably real. And in my less dark years later, whenever I might even possibly begin to doubt the existence of God, I remind myself of what it was like for a year or so back in my early twenties, until God came upon me and saved me. And obviously, I owe a great debt of gratitude.

So that's my first story. And in a sense that experience, I would suggest, was in many ways a reflection of the post–Vatican II era, the sixties and seventies. There was the confusion of society, even in my good little Catholic school, all that goes with maturing in the post-modern or modern world.

Al: And your second experience?

James: The second stage began about two years later. At another level of my personality, I became interested in intellectual things, and I wasn't quite sure how my reason played into all this.

My Uncle Joe had received his bachelor's degree in the late forties from the Jesuits at Le Moyne College in Syracuse, New York. It dawned on me that he might have something to say on matters of faith and reason. I finally got around to asking him, "Do you still have your textbooks from your old Jesuit days?" To which he responded, "Well, yes, they're in boxes in the basement," adding with sweet irony, "those same boxes you tried to throw out a few times when you were cleaning the basement."

My second enduring spiritual experience was this encounter with the intense use of reason, the reason of the Church. Those textbooks on metaphysics and philosophy and theology and all the various branches therein made it abundantly clear to me that, yes, there is faith but there's also reason. Intellectually it was a tremendously saving grace to know that there is order in the cosmos, that there are first principles that govern reality, that truth exists, that theology can help me in decision making and that philosophy will sharpen my thinking skills so I can understand deeply and live skillfully. That's my second stop on my enduring spiritual experiences.

Al: I suppose that calls for number three.

James: And that is when I discovered and began to really understand the wisdom of Christopher Dawson,[5] the great Catholic historian, sociologist and theologian of the Church. What Dawson taught me, which I already knew but didn't appreciate, was *how the faith in an ordered way became clear in culture, clear in the Church* *and clear in the West.* He taught me that religion gives structure and impetus to society.

If I wanted to understand myself and my world, I needed to know how we had gotten off track, lost our spiritual bearings and gotten here. Dawson conveyed to me that it's possible to use faith and reason to go back in time and place and recapture the stages of the great traditions of the Church, so that I could understand today's world in light of that tradition. So he brought it all together in the sense of culture, and I've been running with that ever since.

Al: And that really characterizes your life, doesn't it? Your professional life is focused on humanities and Catholic culture. What is Dawson's status among Catholic historians today?

James: I'm pleased to report that Dawson is becoming well known again! Now, that doesn't mean that Catholic historians across the board have read him at length and grasped his arguments. But as you know, I've been involved with a handful of others in maintaining the tradition of Dawson's thought. It's becoming evident that people are recognizing his existence, reading him and returning to his wonderful insight of the importance of religion to culture and of Roman Catholicism to the West. He is growing in stature once again. More conferences, more people, more programs center on his thought. He's more in vogue today than he's been for probably forty years.

Al: We should get the governing council of the European Union to read Dawson.[6]

James: [Chuckling] Well, the pope suggested they might look in such a direction. His point for our European Union friends is that you can't make good public policy today without knowing from whence you came.

Al: So your story can be called "God, Reason and Christopher Dawson."

James: And in that order, I might add. It's important to keep the priorities straight.

FATHER PAT EGAN
Raised to New Life

The Paschal mystery has two aspects: by his death, Christ liberates us from sin; by his Resurrection, he opens for us the way to a new life. This new life is above all justification that reinstates us in God's grace, "so that as Christ was raised from the dead by the glory of the Father, we too might walk in newness of life."

—*CCC*, 654, quoting Romans 6:4; see 4:25

Father Pat Egan is beloved in the Kresta family. He forged an indispensable link in the chain of events that led our clan to Ann Arbor and what is now Ave Maria Radio. He was a pillar of strength for us upon the untimely death of my brother Michael. His earthiness and good humor insure that his exhortations to love and good works won't be disregarded as mere pious preachments. I have found him an insightful and compassionate confessor, and two of my sons have loved him as their boxing coach. Father Pat is truly both a fighter and a lover.

He holds degrees from Cambridge University, the Gregorian University in Rome and the London School of Economics. After serving as a pastor in London, he founded the Diocesan Pastoral Center there and was secretary of the Westminster Senate of Priests.

In 1982 Father Pat came to the United States to serve The Word of God community in Ann Arbor, Michigan. He is now the corporate chaplain for Domino's Pizza as well as chaplain for Ave Maria Radio and the Ann Arbor Catholic Men's Movement. His reflections on the daily Gospel readings are titled *Fully Alive* and can be heard on www.avemariaradio.net.

Father Pat: A priest's life is full of surprises. I didn't expect to be living in the States. I didn't expect to be charismatic. And the Lord continues to surprise me.

That's as it should be. If nothing is more certain than death, then is there anything more surprising than the Resurrection? We are a people of the Resurrection, and a large part of my life has been spent coming to terms with Jesus' Resurrection. "By your cross and resurrection you have set us free."[1]

I had a conventional Catholic upbringing: Catholic family, Catholic grade school and high school. My father died in my last year of medical school. The Resurrection wasn't yet real to me, and I mourned very much like a pagan.[2] I was angry. "Why have you taken him?"

Al: Did you affirm the Resurrection in the Creed?

Father Pat: Yes, it came with the rations. But we have this capacity to repeat words without letting them actually hit us.

After my father's death I went on a "make-or-break" retreat at Worth Abbey in Sussex. There I had a deep conversion. Although I had gone through the Catholic process, the faith hadn't become "fully alive" to me before then. I had been "sacramentalized" but not truly evangelized.

Al: What do you mean by a "make-or-break" retreat?

Father Pat: Oh, either this Catholic stuff is true or it isn't. It is either the center of my life or just claptrap for covering over life's rough surfaces. If the latter is true, then the best thing to do is to junk it.

Al: Drop it all and get on with your life. Was this a private retreat?

Father Pat: Yes. The abbey was a beautiful place. A couple of my friends from Cambridge regularly visited it, and that's why I had the connection. You could join in the life of the monks. They were very British, so they left you alone a lot and didn't ask intrusive questions.

But I got talking with one of them, and he asked, "Did you pray for your father?"

I said, "Of course I prayed for my father. I said prayers for him every night."

He looked at me and said quietly, "Catholics don't say prayers, Catholics pray prayers." Fifty years later I even remember the tone of his voice.

During that retreat the lights went on. On Monday I had a skeptical frame of mind; on Friday I emerged in love with Jesus. There were no lightning bolts, no Technicolor visions, no audible words from heaven. All I knew was that something changed in me. I started really praying prayers instead of saying prayers.

Over the next year I sorted myself out at Cambridge and then joined the monastery. There I learned to pray the psalms and other Scriptures, but I still had only a notional faith in the Resurrection.

Al: I suppose you are contrasting a notional faith in the Resurrection with a tangible taste of it?

Father Pat: Yes. The Easter Vigil was still something I just did. The Church had recently changed the rite, restoring it to its rightful place as the climax of the liturgical year. Before that the pastor and a few altar servers who could be relied upon to get up at six in the morning would do some things at the front door of the church with fire and water. That was about all, or so it seemed to me at the time.

When I went to the seminary, however, I was introduced to a book that changed my life. It was by a German Redemptorist named François-Xavier Durrwell, and it was called *Christ Our Passover: The Indispensable Role of Resurrection in Our Salvation*.[3] Between that book and going to the new Easter Vigil several times to serve the Mass for the religious at the seminary, it all came together. Suddenly I *knew* rather than just supposed or believed that Christ was alive. I saw the centrality of the Resurrection to our faith.

The sheer, for lack of a better word, "physicality" of the Resurrection hit me. It wasn't just a spiritual resurrection or mere belief in the immortality of the soul. I've never seen someone who had died eat a piece of fish, but the apostles did. I've never put my fingers into his open wounds, but Thomas did. And with that the whole human perspective of life changed.[4]

Al: It changes because our destiny is light not darkness, life not death. Now, was this prior to your ordination?

Father Pat: Yes. This was probably during my novitiate, very early on in my training for the priesthood.

The next step was to get through seminary and get ordained. Then I went to one parish with a very good liturgist and a very good youth club. We had a lot of fun and a lot of impact on people's lives.

Eventually I was asked to start a retreat center for the diocese. There we tried to take more seriously the restoration of the Easter Vigil. We did what we called the Easter Gather. It was a retreat for young people built around the liturgies of Holy Thursday, Good Friday, Holy Saturday and Easter Sunday. It ended with a huge vigil Mass and then an all-night party. The Sunday morning Mass came to be called "the hangover Mass," for the people who one way or another were still hanging over from the night before.

The retreat was tremendously powerful. There were two football linebacker types who came every year. One of them had a cousin who was a dwarf. When we sang "I Will Raise Him Up," these linebacker sorts always picked this kid up and put him on their shoulders. It really brought home the physicality of the Resurrection.

Al: So the power of the Resurrection became real for you. When did you come to a similar appreciation of Pentecost?

Father Pat: That came a little bit later. I think the Holy Spirit tends to be the forgotten member of the Trinity. Objectively we receive him in baptism and confirmation, but we don't expect him to transform our lives from within.

I was looking for power as I did retreat work with young people. Every time we did one, they'd shortly return and ask if we could do a renewal. We couldn't get people into a sustained flight. The spiritual "lift" would soon wear off.

Al: The rain would come and fill them up, but they kept leaking.

Father Pat: Yes. I was looking to keep them filled. I needed to know why people leaked. Why did they lose their conversions so quickly after the retreat? Something was missing. We didn't seem to have the pizzazz or sharing or evangelism of the early Church.

I'd done some sociology, and really, Karl Marx was a very smart guy.[5] He analyzed the notion of power in society: who had it, who used it and for whom. Suddenly I asked, "Where is the Church's power?" The Church's power is the Holy Spirit.

Al: You are certainly the only person that I have ever talked to who gives Karl Marx credit for leading him into the Catholic charismatic renewal.

Father Pat: Well, I won't take that too far. But Marx forced me to think about forms of power.

Later I reluctantly went to a charismatic meeting, during which some people prayed over me. As I was leaving someone said, "Don't do anything different when you get home." So in the best toffee-nosed British way I said, "Of course not."

But when I got home, my prayer life just took off. Texts started leaping out of the Scriptures, as though highlighted, for preaching. People began listening to my preaching in a new way and responding more clearly.

I had received the baptism of the Holy Spirit. So I found myself joining the Catholic charismatic renewal and eventually a covenant community that had international branches. I came to Ann Arbor for a year's training and planned to return to evangelize in London. God had other plans. Surprise—I'm still in the States.

Al: Many of us believe the Creed as truth but would like to experience it as reality. What do you suggest we do?

Father Pat: You have to come before the Lord in emptiness and say, "I believe; help my unbelief" (Mark 9:24). You have to live your faith so as to be as convinced as the apostles were. Those timid country hicks from Galilee were filled with the Holy Spirit, and they took on the supreme court of Israel. We have to invite the Holy Spirit into our lives to give us confidence. The Spirit is given to bear witness to Jesus (see John 15:26; 16:13–15), to preach the resurrected Christ to us and enable us to live his message.

You can't be fully alive without a firm conviction in the Resurrection. The Resurrection is not just the confirming miracle that proves Jesus was right after all. Rather it confers upon us a new way of life with a new horizon. It bestows on us a new power to accomplish Christ's will in the world and in our lives. It gives us a new way of being in the world. It changes everything.

We suffer a little bit from individualism these days. The Resurrection is a corporate event. We've got to have this corporate vision that one day Jesus Christ will be all and all. The whole redeemed humanity will be brought together and presented to the Father. We must maintain the vertical view of the beauty of God as well as this horizontal view of the wholeness of the human family.

All this has come to me from having what I call a resurrected mind in the power of the Holy Spirit. Jesus' resurrection truly brings new life.

A Historical Survey of Personal Testimony in the Service of the Gospel
By Doctor John Love

John Love completed his doctoral work at the Pontifical University of St. Thomas Aquinas in Rome, Italy, in 2005, specializing in spirituality. His doctoral work developed the eucharistic theology of Saint John of the Cross. Over the last three years he has published ten books, articles and reviews on topics in spirituality, vocations and personal and social morality. Currently Doctor Love serves as an assistant professor of systematics at Mount St. Mary's Seminary in Emmitsburg, Maryland, where he lives with his wife and three children.

It may seem that a collection of personal testimonies smacks of revivalist movements of the nineteenth and twentieth centuries and has no place in Catholic spiritual tradition. Nothing could be further from the truth. From Genesis to today, saints have shared their personal stories in order to recommend the way of God in words and deeds. Personal testimony is an integral, *Catholic* (in both senses of "universally used" and "characteristic of the Catholic Church") tool of evangelization.

Pertinent here are two commands that God gave Abraham, "our father in faith": first, to leave his land and people for the Promised Land; second, to use circumcision as the sign of God's covenant (see

Genesis 12; 17). Abraham fulfilled these commands. It seems impossible, however, for him to have simply moved his entire household without some word of explanation—a testimony of his encounter with Yahweh. Even if an ancient tribal chieftain could suddenly uproot his family without disclosing his reasons, urging circumcision upon them would have required some pretty convincing testimony!

Showing God's mighty works through the telling of story is the essence of our records of the Exodus, Joshua's possession of the land, the book of Psalms, the wisdom of Proverbs and the exhortations of the prophets. From Samson's personal triumphs to the theatrics of Elijah to Samuel's calling and ministry through the stories of the great kings David and Solomon, the biblical authors teach us how to live (and how *not* to live) by stories of God's interactions with his people.

The Gospels are mostly comprised of episodic narrations of personal encounters with God in and through Christ.[1] From Mary's meeting with Gabriel to the prophetic dreams of Joseph and the Magi, to the call of the apostles, to the conversion and healing of many, to the witnesses of the Resurrection, the evangelists crafted their portraits of Christ with personal testimonies, as an artist would weave a grand and beautiful tapestry of many and varied threads. At the center stands the towering hero of the Gospels, who came to "*bear witness* to the truth" (John 18:37) that "God is love" (1 John 4:8) and that we should love one another as he has loved us (see John 15:12).

Peter's apostolic preaching began on Pentecost with the personal witness of the apostles to the life, death and resurrection of Jesus (see Acts 3:15). Paul began his proclamation of the gospel by also referring to the witness of the apostles (Acts 13:31). When he was arrested in Jerusalem, he shared with the people his personal testimony, especially the story of his encounter with Jesus on the road to Damascus and his subsequent commission to preach the gospel to the gentiles

(Acts 22:1–21). In his letters Paul defended his apostolic status, which was based on his personal meeting with Jesus (Romans 1:1–2; 15:14–20; Galatians 1:11–24; Ephesians 1:1–2; 3:7–9). In addition, Saint Paul frequently used his personal experiences to punctuate his presentation of the Good News (2 Corinthians 11:21–12:10; Galatians 4:12–14; Philippians 1:12–15; Colossians 1:24–29; 1 Thessalonians 2:1–12).

This practice of personal testimony didn't end with the apostles.

MARTYRS TO MISSIONARIES

Saint Ignatius of Antioch (who died sometime between AD 98 and 117, according to different sources) followed in Saint Paul's footsteps, both in being taken to Rome in chains and martyred there and in the use of personal testimony in letters.[2] In the succeeding century stories of the early martyrs encouraged Christians to face their persecutors. A few examples of written testimony include *The Martyrdom of Polycarp* (d. 155), *Acts of Perpetua and Felicitas* (d. 203) and *The Life and Passion of Cyprian* (d. 248). Saint Justin Martyr wrote in his Second *Apology* that the witness of the martyrs led him to become a Christian.[3] Certainly Justin was not alone, as Tertullian's famous phrase, written in 197, indicates: "The blood of the martyrs is the seed of the Church."[4] Many Fathers of the Church, including Saint Basil (d. 379), Saint John Chrysostom (d. 407), Saint Augustine (d. 430), Saint Peter Chrysologus (d. 450) and Saint John Damascene (d. 787), persistently pointed to the martyrs as they preached the Word of God to the Church.

When Roman persecutions evaporated after Constantine made Christianity legal in 313, the use of personal testimony in spreading the gospel did not. In the middle of the fourth century, Saint Athanasius wrote *The Life of St. Antony*, disclosing the exploits of perhaps the most famous monk, who left the bustle and security of Roman-era cities to do spiritual combat with devils in the Middle Eastern deserts. Saint Augustine wrote in his *Confessions* that Saint Antony's life, as portrayed by Saint Athanasius, sparked the flame of desire in his heart to reject sin and turn to God.[5]

Augustine's *Confessions* is without question one of the most personally revealing, theologically penetrating, rhetorically ingenious and emotionally moving books ever written. It is evangelization through personal testimony par excellence.

While the Roman world of Saint Augustine disintegrated, Saint Patrick worked to bring the light of Christ to a distant land on the northwest frontier of Roman territory. He used his autobiographical *Confession* to proclaim the gospel. Where Saint Augustine's work is refined and subtle, Saint Patrick's text is unsophisticated and coarse.

These books reflect the circumstances of the two saints, who stood one on each side of a great historical crossroad: the end of Rome and the beginning of Europe. Yet with all the differences between the two men and the two books, the stories of their personal encounters with Christ were means to very successfully win converts to the Church.

Once the Germanic tribes had achieved their political conquest of the Roman state, the sons of Saint Patrick's evangelistic efforts, the Irish missionaries, swept over the European continent, together with other brave bearers of the light of Christ, imbuing the new social order with the Catholic faith. The historical records from this difficult time of transition are sparse, and many extant sources date from significantly after the people and events they describe. Yet the memoirs and biographies that were written inspired countless Christians to seek the prayers of and make pilgrimages to the shrines of Saint Brigid of Kildare (d. 525), Saint Brendan the Navigator (d. 577), Saint Columba (d. 597) and many other saints who helped reclaim Europe for Christ.

In the same epoch Pope Saint Gregory the Great (d. 604) worked tirelessly to fuse the disparate elements of post-Roman society into a cohesive whole: Christendom, united by a common Catholic culture. Among his other contributions, Saint Gregory gave beautiful sermons that combined theological insight with personal anecdotes.

Stories from the lives of the saints were to the medieval centuries what the stories of the martyrs were to the Roman world: In both cases the lives of heroic Christians inspired countless masses to turn away from sin and devote themselves to holiness. The *Book of the Popes* and later the *Golden Legend* spread the fame of popes and saints, respectively, to inspire the faith of Christians everywhere.[6] Moved by these tales, thousands of people left their homes to make spiritual pilgrimages to Rome, Santiago de Compostela (the reputed burial place of the apostle James the Great) and, above all, the Holy Land.

MYSTICS AND MENDICANTS

Mystics have written with vivid imagery about their ultimately indescribable encounters with God, in efforts to share the fruit of their experiences with others.[7] Saint Bernard of Clairvaux's most important mystical text is his four-volume *Commentary on the Song of Songs*, in which he employed a largely allegorical interpretation, setting Christ as the Bridegroom and the Christian as the bride. Bernard's intimate experience of God guided his reflections and led many readers to conversion.

Each possessing their own distinctive emphases and styles, other medieval mystics include Meister Eckhart (d. 1327), John Tauler (d. 1361), Blessed Henry Suso (d. 1366) and Blessed John of Ruysbroeck (d. 1381) (known together as "The Rhineland Mystics"), Saint Bridget of Sweden (d. 1373), Saint Catherine of Siena (d. 1380),

Saint Julian of Norwich (d. 1416) and the anonymous English author of *The Cloud of Unknowing*, dating from the fifteenth century. Remarkably, Christian mystics of every age and situation testify variously to personal encounters with the God who reveals his consummate and personal love for all and invites us into a spousal relationship with him.

The thirteenth century witnessed a new awakening of Christian fervor, marked by the rise of the mendicant orders, particularly the Dominicans and the Franciscans. Saint Dominic (d. 1221) and Saint Francis (d. 1226) preached the gospel with zeal and personal magnetism, which helped their communities explode with adherents and reevangelize the late medieval world. Each founder was considered a saint during his lifetime, and their orders still flourish today with men and women who, like their medieval counterparts, bear witness to Christ at work in the lives of Francis and Dominic.

Not least among medieval saints, Saint Joan of Arc, at the age of thirteen, received revelations from angels and saints telling her to assist the king of France, Charles VII, in the seemingly interminable wars with the English. Saint Joan was eventually granted a military command, and she successfully fought to save her native country from subjugation. Tragically, in 1431 she was captured and executed, at the age of twenty.

Moving into the modern era, Ignatius of Loyola (d. 1556) found inspiration when he read the lives of the saints in 1521, during his convalescence from injuries received in battle. This began his lifelong mission of service to God, the Church and people everywhere. Ignatius wrote his autobiography to share his personal story, and he left *The Spiritual Exercises* to help retreat directors guide searching souls through (ideally) a four-week discernment process to find God's will for their lives. It is clear that the scriptural meditations that comprise the *Exercises* originated with Saint Ignatius's own efforts to discover God's will for his life, once he had renounced his career as a soldier and devoted his life to the Lord.

Saint Teresa of Avila (d. 1582) and Saint John of the Cross (d. 1591) contributed great masterworks in the mystical tradition: Her *Life* and *Interior Castle* and his *Dark Night of the Soul, Spiritual Canticle* and *Living Flame of Love* are all autobiographical. They captivate readers precisely because they explain the love of God from personal experience, not according to principles of theology alone.

GOD'S LOVE REVEALED

In the modern era there have been many saints who received private revelations from Jesus or Mary that the Church officially recognizes as authentically divine in origin. These revelations have enlightened and encouraged the faithful everywhere. Saint Mary Alacoque (d. 1690), for example, received revelations concerning the Sacred Heart of Jesus and his profound and multifaceted love flowing from it. Saint Bernadette Soubirous (d. 1879) was a young and uneducated girl when she received revelations about the Immaculate Conception of Mary. The three children at Fatima, Portugal,—Lucia Dos Santos, Blessed Francisco Marto and Blessed Jacinta Marto—received messages from Mary in 1917 about the necessity of prayer, reparation and consecration, which would lead to peace in the world. Saint Faustina Kowalska (d. 1938) received the message of Divine Mercy in a now-famous image of Christ with red and white rays shooting from his heart and the message "Jesus, I trust in you" inscribed below. All of these visionaries shared their private encounters with the Lord and his mother and so offered the world hope in the midst of atrocities, destruction and global wars.

The close of the nineteenth century saw the deaths of two giants whose personal stories have led to untold conversions. A cloistered Carmelite nun, who died from tuberculosis at age twenty-four, wrote a touching and sweet story about her spiritual journey and the gracious love of God, which exalts the humble and populates the kingdom of God with the "little ones." Saint Thérèse of Lisieux (d. 1897) and her *Story of a Soul* have become enormously popular, and they garnered such high honor that Thérèse was named the thirty-third doctor of the Church.

Venerable John Henry Newman (d. 1890) told of his spiritual journey from evangelicalism to Anglo-Catholicism and then into the Catholic Church in a masterpiece of English prose. His *Apologia Pro Vita Sua* (1865) is acclaimed as one of the most brilliant works of spiritual autobiography.

The twentieth century gave us Dorothy Day's *The Long Loneliness,* Thomas Merton's *Seven Storey Mountain*, Bede Griffiths's *The Golden String* and an explosion of less literary but equally arresting stories. Missionaries and preachers like Bishop Fulton Sheen, Mother Angelica, Father Michael Scanlan, Father Benedict Groeschel, Father John Corapi, Blessed Teresa of Calcutta and Pope John Paul the Great have drawn on their personal experiences, particularly their experiences of suffering, to enlighten, exhort and encourage the world to embrace Christ and his gospel.

Jesus is the personal testimony of the Father made human, and the Holy Spirit is the personal testimony of Christ made available to all generations, so that every race, tongue, nation and time might know God, love him and serve him. It is not just the saints or just the clergy who must bear witness to the gospel; all Christians must imitate Christ, and it is our privilege to testify to the love of God and the salvation he offers us in Christ.

NOTES

Introduction: *Why You May Know More About Reality Than Do Freud, Marx and Dawkins*

1. In 1974 I realized that the Jesus of the New Age movement was not the Jesus of the New Testament. For the next eighteen years I served in various capacities in evangelical Protestant circles, including five years as a pastor of an independent church. From evangelical Protestant teachers I rediscovered Christ's lordship. After that I learned to value and read Scripture as divine revelation, learned the importance and the know-how of personal evangelism, learned how to preach and teach, learned the importance of the church as the body of Christ and much more. My return to the Catholic Church in 1992 represented not a repudiation but a fulfillment of my evangelical Protestant experience. See my chapter "All Detours Lead to Rome" in Patrick Madrid, ed., *Surprised by Truth: 11 Converts Give the Biblical and Historical Reasons for Becoming Catholic* (San Diego: Basilica, 1994).

2. Daniel C. Dennett, "Candidates' Religious Hypocrisy Won't Stand," available at: http://newsweek.washingtonpost.com.

3. Because of differences in theology and doctrine, some people dismiss "experiences of the transcendent" as hopelessly inconsistent. To the contrary, spiritual experiences are so consistent across cultures, across time and across faiths that psychiatrists and neurophysiologists are trying to find some core biological explanation. I distinguish between the raw experience of God and the doctrines that flow from and seek to formulate that experience. If experience is to be communicated, it necessarily requires interpretation.

As a Catholic I accept the teaching authority of the Catholic Church and the apostolic tradition as the foundational control on interpretation. But I'm convinced that the closer we get to the actual experience of the divine, the more similar is the language. For example, one of the great divides between world religions is the question of whether or not God is personal. Judaism, Christianity and, for the most part, Islam teach a personal God; Hinduism,

Buddhism and Jainism teach an impersonal God. This "contradiction" begins to break down when we consider the difference between religious experience and religious belief, encounter with God and doctrine about him. At the level of common experience rather than formal doctrine, Hindus frequently experience God as intelligence or love, as in, for instance, Paramahansa Yogananda's *Autobiography of a Yogi* (Nevada City, Calif: Crystal Clarity, 2005). Setting aside my deep theological differences with his Hinduism, it is not difficult to read his story as a remarkable series of coincidences, leadings, promptings and interior apprehensions of God as providential and intelligent.

Swami Vivekananda (1863–1902), envoy to the famed 1893 World Parliament of Religions, was one of the most influential spiritual leaders of the Vedanta philosophy and the chief disciple of the legendary Ramakrishna (1836–1886). He taught that *Brahman*, the ultimate reality of Hinduism, was connected to the *Logos* of Christianity or Greek philosophy. *Brahman* is pure intelligence. I would argue that common experience of God is not impersonal. God may be "beyond personality," as C.S. Lewis put it, but he certainly isn't less than personal. We have an I/Thou relationship with ultimate reality. For an insightful analysis of some of the problems between Eastern and Western religious experience and belief, see "The Unity and Diversity of Religions: The Place of Christianity in the History of Religions" in Cardinal Joseph Ratzinger, *Truth and Tolerance: Christian Belief and World Religions*, Henry Taylor, trans. (San Francisco: Ignatius, 2004), pp. 15–44.

4. An exception to this observation is Doctor Regis Martin, who was inflamed by Saint Thomas of Aquinas's "Third Way." (He tells his story in part seven.) But notice that his grasp of this argument seized him at the deepest level of his being. It was a realization, not merely a reason. A study of Saint Paul's defense of the gospel in the book of Acts and his letters shows him reasoning, arguing, persuading, defending, teaching as well as sharing his own experience of Christ on the road to Damascus. See Acts 14:6–20; 17; 22:1–21; 26; Romans 1:18–32; 2 Corinthians 10:5; Philippians 1:7. See F.F. Bruce, *The Defense of the Gospel in the New Testament* (Grand Rapids: Eerdmans, 1982). Again, one need not accept the false dilemma of rational religion versus spiritual experience.

5. John Stuart Mill, *Three Essays on Religion* (New York: Henry Holt, 1874), p. 219.

6. Psychology professor Paul Vitz develops this idea in *Faith of the Fatherless: The Psychology of Atheism* (Dallas: Spence, 2000). See also Calvinist theologian R.C. Sproul's *The Psychology of Atheism* (1974), revised as *If There Is a God, Why Are There Atheists?: A Surprising Look at the Psychology of Atheism* (Minneapolis: Bethany Fellowship, 1978). On a novel approach to atheistic critiques of Christianity, see Merold Westphal, *Suspicion and Faith: The Religious Uses of Modern Atheism* (New York: Fordham University Press, 1999).

7. "Special Report: Exploring Religious America," *Religion and Ethics NewsWeekly*, April 26, 2002, www.pbs.org.

8. Dean Hamer, "Excerpt: 'The God Gene,'" http://abcnews.go.com, July 21, 2008.

9. Charles Raven, *Jesus and the Gospel of Love* (London: Hodder and Stoughton, 1931), p. 73, as quoted in D. Elton Trueblood, *The Trustworthiness of Religious Experience* (Richmond, Ind.: Friends United, 1988), p. 39.

10. See André Ravier, s.j., *As a Little Child: The Mysticism of "Little Children" and of "Those Who are Like Them"* (New York: Alba House, 1998).

11. See D. Elton Trueblood, *The Knowledge of God* (New York: Harper, 1939), pp. 144–152.

12. See Ronald A. Knox, *Enthusiasm: A Chapter in the History of Religion: With Special Reference to the XVII and XVIII Centuries* (South Bend, Ind.: University of Notre Dame Press, 1994). Catholic philosopher Jacques Maritain distinguished between the provisional experience of God we have in this world and the beatific vision promised us after we are purged of disordered self-love. In the beatific vision we know him as he is in himself. No image, idea or created thing comes between us. On earth, however, it is possible for the faithful to experience an approximation of that vision. In faith we long to know God. While faith doesn't yet see God in his essence or fullness, the faithful can have an authentic but not exhaustive knowledge of God through adhering to what God has revealed of himself.

> [A]ll purely intellectual knowledge of God, short of the Beatific Vision, even though it be absolutely true, absolutely certain, and constitute an

authentic wisdom, desirable above all things, is still irreparably defective, lacking due proportion to the object known and signified, in its very manner of grasping and signifying.... Here below, intellect can enter the realm that lies beyond all method only by a renunciation-of-knowing in which God's Spirit, by making use of the connaturality of charity and the effects produced in affection by Divine Union, grants the soul a loving experience of that very being which no notion approximates or can approximate. (Jacques Maritain, "The Grandeur and Poverty of Metaphysics," in Donald and Idella Gallagher, eds., *A Maritain Reader* [Garden City, N.Y.: Doubleday, 1966], pp. 48–49).

See Jacques Maritain, *The Degrees of Knowledge* (New York: Scribner's, 1938), p. 308; *The Range of Reason* (New York: Scribner's, 1942), p. 24. In *Approaches to God* (New York: Colliers, 1962, pp. 108–119, Maritain provides a digest of relevant passages from Saint Thomas Aquinas's *Summa Theologica*.

13. Joseph Ratzinger, *Christianity and the Crisis of Cultures* (San Francisco: Ignatius, 2006), p. 91.

ONE: DAMASCUS ROAD
Norma McCorvey: Roe No More
1. Roe No More Ministry, www.leaderu.com/norma

2. Father Frank Pavone is president and founder of Priests for Life. His story is told in part seven of this volume. Father Edward Robinson, O.P., of St. Albert's Dominican Priory in Dallas, Texas, is editor of www.unbornperson.com. He is well known throughout Dallas for his pro-life leadership.

3. Jehovah's Witnesses regard the Catholic Church as a pagan religion that has turned the worship of the true God into the worship of devils.

4. Philip "Flip" Benham (1948—), whom Norma ridiculed as Flip "Venom," was in 1995 the national director of Operation Rescue. His headquarters were right next to the abortion clinic where Norma was working. On August 8, 1995, Benham baptized Norma in a backyard swimming pool. The pictures were widely circulated in the press.

5. In her book *Won By Love*, Norma writes that when she first met Emily Mackey, she told her, "I like little kids, and I don't like anybody mistreating

them," to which Emily responded, "Then why are you letting the little ones die inside?" (Norma McCorvey with Gary Thomas, *Won by Love: Norma McCorvey, Jane Roe of Roe v. Wade, Speaks Out for the Unborn as She Shares Her New Conviction For Life* [Nashville: Thomas Nelson, 1997], p. 91). Norma's heart was further softened when she learned that Emily had almost been aborted. Ronda Mackey's fiancé and prospective in-laws urged her to abort in the first trimester. After saying she would abort, she recalled the emotional devastation that had followed a friend's abortion and refused to follow through. Emily lived and became the heartrending face of abortion to Norma.

6. Doctor Morris Sheats founded Hillcrest Church in Dallas, Texas, in 1984. He pastored it until 2003, when he left to found Heritage Church in the Dallas suburb of Richardson.

7. See David Currie, *Born Fundamentalist, Born Again Catholic* (San Francisco: Ignatius, 1996).

Steve Ray: In the Company of the Great King and All His Family
1. It's been said that this hymn has touched more hearts and influenced more people for Christ than any other song ever written (see Kenneth W. Osbeck, *101 Hymn Stories* [Grand Rapids: Kregel, 1982], p. 146). The text was born out of the suffering of an invalid woman, Charlotte Elliott (1789–1871). She resisted the gospel until a traveling evangelist persuaded her with the words: "You must come just as you are, a sinner, to the Lamb of God that taketh away the sin of the world." When evangelist Billy Graham published his autobiography in 1997, he named it after the hymn that best character-ized his crusade rallies, "Just as I Am."

Monica Migliorino Miller: That Hidden Face
1. *Suddenly Last Summer,* by Tennessee Williams, is a one-act play that opened off Broadway in January 1958 and was later adapted as a feature film. It is considered one of Williams's bleakest but most poetic works, incorpo-rating topics including insanity, homosexuality, cannibalism and hypocrisy. The character of Sister Felicity is often portrayed as naively virtuous.

2. Ida Friederike Gorres, *The Hidden Face: A Study of St. Thérèse of Lisieux*, second rev. ed. (San Francisco: Ignatius, 2003).

3. St. Joseph Monastery in Des Plaines, Illinois, is home to the contemplative Order of Discalced Carmelites.

Ralph Martin: No Retreat From the Truth
1. The world, the flesh and the devil.
- The world is the fallen created order, including godless society and culture (see 1 John 2:15).
- The flesh includes fallen human impulses, bent toward evil (see Romans 7).
- The devil is a personal agent of evil who, together with demons, uses the world and the flesh to involve humans in rebellion against God.

2. Secular existentialism dominated the salon and café scene of Europe with its novels and plays during the middle of the twentieth century. Although there are religious versions of it, existentialism is usually considered atheistic, emphasizing the solitary individual alone in the world with no objective moral guidelines. Ironically, it is usually traced back to the Christian Danish thinker Søren Kierkegaard (1813–1855).

3. The word *cursillo* is Spanish for "little course." The Cursillo movement is directed toward introducing or renewing a person's sense of Christ as the center of the spiritual life. The movement grew out of an idea, first advanced at the Monastery of San Honorato, on the island of Majorca off the coast of Spain, to teach Catholics the importance of Christ in their lives. It has grown into an international movement.

4. Ignatius of Loyola (1491–1556), founder of the Society of Jesus (the Jesuits), formulated a set of precepts, called the Spiritual Exercises, to help people draw near to God.

5. Teresa Tomeo, *Noise: How Our Media-saturated Culture Dominates Lives and Dismantles Families* (West Chester, Pa.: Ascension, 2007). See chapter three.

TWO: ASLEEP IN THE LIGHT
Patrick Madrid: Not Surprised by Truth
1. *Surprised by Truth: 11 Converts Give the Biblical and Historical Reasons for Becoming Catholic* (San Diego: Basilica, 1994); *Surprised by Truth 2: 15 Men and Women Give the Biblical and Historical Reasons for Becoming Catholic* (Manchester, N.H.: Sophia Institute, 2000); *Surprised by Truth 3: 10 More*

Converts Give the Biblical and Historical Reasons for Becoming Catholic (Manchester, N.H.: Sophia Institute, 2002) were all edited and coauthored by Patrick Madrid. Al Kresta's testimony is included in the first volume.

2. Karl Keating is founder and president of Catholic Answers, an international apologetics and evangelization ministry. Karl has authored a number of books, including the best-selling *Catholicism and Fundamentalism: The Attack on "Romanism" by "Bible Christians"* (San Francisco: Ignatius, 1988).

Russell Shaw: The Work of God, the Work of Life
1. *Opus Dei* (Latin for "Work of God") describes itself as "a Catholic institution founded by Saint Josemaría Escrivá...[whose] mission is to help people turn their work and daily activities into occasions for growing closer to God, for serving others, and for improving society." It was founded in 1928 and has about eighty-seven thousand members in eighty countries. See: http://www.opusdei.org/.

2. An allusion to the warped, murderous character in Dan Brown's *The Da Vinci Code*. Opus Dei has no monks.

John Martignoni: It's Real!
1. The history of Christian spirituality contains an enormous number of unusual but personally compelling experiences. Catholic teaching has generated a vast literature on private revelation and mystical experience, with many warnings and insistence on discernment of spirits. However, "simple, sudden and illuminating views of faith, which [enable] one to understand in a higher manner not novelties, but the truths admitted by the Church...[are] a very precious grace, which should be very carefully welcomed and utilized" (from "Private Revelation," in *Catholic Encyclopedia*, 1917, online edition by New Advent, www.newadvent.org).

THREE: THE INVISIBLE HAND
Teresa Tomeo: There Are No Accidents
1. Jennifer Granholm, a member of a Detroit-area Catholic parish, is governor of Michigan. Her advocacy of abortion rights and support for partial-birth abortion caused great controversy among Michigan Catholics during her 2004 campaign. John Kerry, a member of a Catholic parish in Georgetown, outside Washington, D.C., was the Democratic presidential

nominee in 2004. His candidacy also caused controversy among Catholics, including a debate over whether or not he should be denied Communion because of his advocacy of abortion rights.

Paul Thigpen: From Optimism to Hope
1. François-Marie Arouet, "Voltaire" (1694–1778), is best known today as the author of the satirical philosophical tale *Candide*. A prolific author and playwright, he tried to discredit Christianity as a façade of impostures. He is often counted with the *philosophes*, who frequently were atheists, but he stopped short of atheism. The Enlightenment, or "Age of Reason," is the period of Western intellectual history that runs from the late seventeenth through the eighteenth centuries. It rejected revealed religion and trusted reason alone as authoritative. Other common beliefs included the perfectibility of man, radical social reform and belief in individual rights. Institutions like the Church and monarchy lost considerable authority during this era. See Colin Brown, *Christianity & Western Thought, Volume 1: From the Ancient World to the Age of Enlightenment* (Downers Grove, Ill.: InterVarsity Press, 1990), p. 289.

Chris Godfrey: Who's Calling This Play?
1. The New York Jets front-four defense, led by defensive ends Gastineau and Klecko and defensive tackles Lyons and Salaam (born Larry Faulk), terrorized opponents during the early 1980s.

2. Then head coach, Bart Starr had quarterbacked the Green Bay Packers (1956–1971) and was MVP of the first two Super Bowls. Vince Lombardi's Packers won NFL championships in the 1961, 1962, 1965, 1966 and 1967 seasons. After three years as assistant coach for the Packers, Starr became head coach in 1975.

3. Vince Lombardi (1913–1970) was the legendary head coach of the Green Bay Packers from 1959 to 1967, winning five league championships during his nine years. After his death in 1970, the NFL began awarding the Vince Lombardi Trophy each year to the winning team of the Super Bowl. It is the NFL's most prestigious award. During the 1960s, when many traditional institutions and beliefs were under attack, Lombardi's blunt talk about commitment to God, family, leadership, authority and character won him a wide audience of admirers as well as critics. Vince Lombardi remained a committed Catholic throughout his life.

Marcus Grodi: Our God Is a Sovereign God

1. Especially in Mark's Gospel, Jesus maintains an element of secrecy about himself and his work. The term "messianic secret" is derived from the classic study of William Wrede in 1901.

2. Saint Thomas More (1478–1535), statesman, lawyer, chancellor of England, is best remembered for his refusal to assent to Henry VIII's outrageous claim to be supreme head of the Church of England. This refusal ended his political career and led to his execution for treason.

3. *The Testament* by John Grisham (New York: Island, 1999) is a legal thriller. Grisham (born February 8, 1955) is an American writer who worked as a lawyer and politician. As of 2008 his books have sold over 235 million copies worldwide. He describes himself as a "moderate Baptist."

FOUR: ONE SMALL STEP

Sister Ann Shields: God's Power Is Made Perfect in Weakness

1. The Second Vatican Council was held from October 11, 1962, to December 8, 1965. It was the twenty-first ecumenical ("whole world") council of the Catholic Church and certainly the single most important religious event of the twentieth century. One of its sixteen documents, *Perfectae Caritati* (Decree on the Renewal of Religious Life, October 28, 1965), called religious orders to rediscover their founding charisms (inspirations). It also called for development of new forms of religious life. Ironically, the number of sisters and nuns in America has steeply declined since the end of the council. In 1965 sisters numbered 185,000 in more than 500 orders. By 2005 the total had dropped by more than half, to 68,963, and of those fewer than 6,000 were under the age of fifty. On the other hand, a number of new orders oriented to the spirit and word of Vatican II have emerged, including the Servants of God's Love. See Ann Carey, *Sisters in Crisis: The Tragic Unraveling of Women's Religious Communities* (Huntington, Ind.: Our Sunday Visitor, 1997) and Alan Schreck, *Vatican II: The Crisis and the Promise* (Cincinnati: Servant, 2005).

2. Father Michael Scanlan, past president and now chancellor of the Franciscan University of Steubenville, is a well-known conference speaker and author. His books include *The Truth About Trouble: How Hard Times Can Draw You Closer to God* (Cincinnati: Servant, 2005) and *What Does*

God Want: A Practical Guide to Making Decisions (Huntington, Ind.: Our Sunday Visitor, 1997).

Joseph Pearce: Finding True Freedom
1. *Bulldog* was the newspaper of the Young National Front. Joseph was also editor of *Nationalism Today*, a "higher brow" journal of opinion.

2. Distributism attempts to create a third way between large corporate capitalism and large governmental socialism. Advocates for distributism claim that it best embodies the thought of the Catholic social encyclicals, such as Pope Leo XIII's *Rerum Novarum*, Pope Pius XI's *Quadragesimo Anno* and even Pope John Paul II's *Centesimus Annus*. What should be distributed under distributism? Ownership of the means of production. As Chesterton put it: "Too much capitalism does not mean too many capitalists, but too few capitalists" (cited at: www.basicincome.com). Distributism considers the family rather than the individual to be the fundamental unit of society and tries to avoid the extremisms of individualism and statism. See Joseph Pearce, *Small Is Still Beautiful: Economics as if Families Mattered* (Chicago: Intercollegiate Studies Institute, 2000).

3. Though *Orthodoxy* and *The Everlasting Man* are the Chesterton titles most people first read, Joseph read Chesterton's *Outline of Sanity*, a robust explanation of distributism, and an essay, "Reflections on a Rotten Apple," from a collection of Chesterton titled *The Well and the Shallows*. Because Chesterton's faith and social thought were so well integrated, Joseph was unable to get to Chesterton's political and economic thought without also encountering a constant case for the Christian faith.

Robert Lockwood: Mass Disturbance
1. The Way-Back Machine is an allusion to the time-transport device utilized by the dog Mr. Peabody and his boy Sherman to facilitate their historical adventures on arguably the greatest cartoon show of all time, *Rocky and Bullwinkle*.

2. John Bertram Phillips (1906–1982) was a Bible translator, writer and clergyman in the Church of England.

William Donohue: Caught by Catholicism
1. Archbishop Fulton John Sheen (1895–1979) authored over ninety books

and was the best-known religious media figure during the early years of the Cold War. He hosted *Life Is Worth Living*, which won him an Emmy in 1952.

2. John Stuart Mill (1806–1873) is known as a philosopher of classical libertarianism as well as utilitarianism, both of which John Paul II regularly criticized. Mill had proposed the "harm principle" as the criterion for individual and governmental intervention. According to Mill, we can only interfere with the liberty of another in order to prevent harm to ourselves or another. Pope John Paul II regarded this as too narrow a basis for intervention.

3. John Paul II wrote that all mistaken views about freedom "are at one in lessening or even denying the *dependence of freedom on truth*" (*Veritatis Splendor*, 34). According to Christian faith, "only the freedom which submits to the Truth leads the human person to his true good. The good of the person is to be in the Truth and to *do* the Truth" (84). Human beings are free precisely when they submit to the truth. See J. Michael Miller, ed., *The Encyclicals of John Paul II* (Huntington, Ind.: Our Sunday Visitor, 1996), p. 656.

SIX: FAMILY TIES
Jennifer Roback Morse: He Does as He Wills

1. An annulment is a decree of nullity, not a "Catholic divorce." In fact, it is the very opposite of a divorce, which tears apart what God joined. An annulment is simply a statement that, after looking at a wide range of details, the Church recognizes that no marriage in fact took place. There was, of course, a civil marriage but not a marriage in the Catholic understanding.

2. George Mason University is a public university with its primary campus in Fairfax, Virginia. It is named after the founding father George Mason (1725–1792), who along with James Madison is called a "father of the Bill of Rights."

3. Leonard Liggio (1933—) is a classical liberal author, a research professor of law at George Mason University and the executive vice president of the Atlas Economic Research Foundation in Fairfax, Virginia. See his article "The Heritage of the Spanish Scholastics," http://www.acton.org.

4. Cornelius Michael Buckley, *When Jesuits Were Giants: Louis-Marie Ruellan, S.J. (1846–1885) and Contemporaries* (San Francisco: Ignatius, 1999).

5. See Congregation for the Doctrine of the Faith, *Donum vitae,* Instruction on Respect for Human Life in Its Origin, 1987; Pope Paul VI, *Humanae Vitae;* John B. Shea, "The moral status of in vitro fertilization (IVF) Biology and method," *Catholic Insight,* January/February 2003.

6. See Pope John Paul II, *Mulieris Dignatatem;* also "Man Becomes the Image of God by Communion of Persons," General Audience of Wednesday, November 14, 1979, available at: http://www.ewtn.com.

Doug Keck: His Grace Is Sufficient
1. Marriage Encounter began in 1952 in Barcelona, Spain, as a Catholic marriage renewal program. It is now worldwide in scope and offers various "expressions" for other Christian traditions.

2. *Refrigerator mother* was a term used especially in the mid-twentieth century to label mothers of autistic children. These mothers were thought to be frigid, distant and rejecting and thus unable to provide the necessary maternal warmth for their child's healthy development. The tide began turning in 1964 with the publication of psychologist Bernard Rimland's *Infantile Autism: The Syndrome and Its Implications for a Neural Theory of Behavior.* Rimland himself had an autistic son and thus had the academic credentials and moral authority to take on the "refrigerator mother" hypothesis. By the late 1970s the term was being discredited. New theories about the causes of autism were being proposed. But the term persists in some circles.

3. Second Corinthians 12:7–10 contains Saint Paul's discussion of his "thorn in the flesh." Whatever it was (and commentators are uncertain), it became spiritually burdensome for him. However, through God Paul met the challenge. "Three times I begged the Lord about this, that it should leave me; but he said to me, 'My grace is sufficient for you, for my power is made perfect in weakness.' I will all the more gladly boast of my weaknesses, that the power of Christ may rest upon me" (verses 8–9).

4. The manna that was the supernatural source of food for the children of Israel in their forty years of wilderness wanderings is often used as an illustration of God's grace. It was given daily, to be sufficient for the day; the people gathered it daily, and they were warned not to hoard more than was necessary for the day, otherwise it would spoil. (See Exodus 16; Numbers 11:6–9).

Jeff Cavins: Redeem the Time
1. Father Michael Scanlan was at that time chancellor of the Franciscan University of Steubenville. He is renowned not only for his educational work but also as a powerful evangelist and spiritual author.

2. This is one of the most loved biblical passages. The Lord tells Moses to teach Aaron and his sons this liturgical formula for blessing the Israelites.

SEVEN: WHAT YOU WIN THEM WITH IS WHAT YOU WIN THEM TO
Father Frank Pavone: Rescue Those Being Led to Slaughter
1. There are many spokes on the pro-life wheel: crisis pregnancy centers, educational organizations, lobbying groups, legislative counsels, sidewalk counselors, march organizers and so forth. "Rescue" is direct action and considered controversial. On a given day, at a given hour, rescuers nonviolently seat themselves in front of an abortionist's door in sufficient numbers to make access almost impossible. They remain seated, singing or praying. As women scheduled for abortions arrive, trained sidewalk counselors offer spiritual, financial or emotional assistance. Rescue is not a protest or civil disobedience in order to change laws or make political statements. Rather Rescuers believe that by placing themselves between the unborn and the abortionist's instruments of destruction, mothers will reconsider their choice to kill. It is analogous to trespassing onto a neighbor's property if you believe a child is about to be injured by a violent parent. See Randall A. Terry, *Operation Rescue* (New Kensington, Pa.: Whitaker, 1988).

Regis Martin: A Man of Fiery Being
1. Frederick "Fritz" D. Wilhelmsen (1923–1996) has been described by Emory University's Patrick Allitt, in *Catholic Intellectuals and Conservative Politics in America,* as the "most brilliantly acute intellect" among his generation of intellectual conservatives. Wilhelmsen took on philosophy, political theory, religious inquiry and cultural criticism on four continents. He was the editor of several seminal journals and author of sixteen books and more than 250 articles. See the tribute "Christendom's Troubadour: Frederick D. Wilhelmsen" by James Lehrberger, O. CIST, in *Intercollegiate Review*, Spring 1996, p. 52.

2. *El Escorial* is the Royal Monastery of San Lorenzo, located about thirty miles northwest of Madrid. Built by Philip II (r. 1556–1598), its complex

served as a monastery and a Spanish royal palace. At present it is an Augustinian monastery.

3. Nihilism is the view that nothingness is the final reality. All human aspirations for love, meaning and significance are ultimately unfulfillable. This negation of all being or value often leads to despair.

4. Saint Thomas Aquinas's "Third Way" in *Medieval Sourcebook*, http://www.fordham.edu. *Handbook of Christian Apologetics* unpacks the argument:

 1. If something exists, there must exist what it takes for that thing to exist.
 2. The universe—the collection of beings in space and time—exists.
 3. Therefore, there must exist what it takes for the universe to exist.
 4. What it takes for the universe to exist cannot exist within the universe or be bounded by space and time.
 5. Therefore, what it takes for the universe to exist must transcend both space and time.

(Peter Kreeft and Ronald K. Tacelli, *Handbook of Christian Apologetics: Hundreds of Answers to Crucial Questions* [Downers Grove, Ill: InterVarsity Press, 1994], p. 61.)

5. Josef Seifert is head of the International Academy of Philosophy in Vaduz, Liechtenstein.

6. Father W. Norris Clarke, S.J., taught philosophy at Fordham University from 1955 to 1985.

7. Cited in Josef Pieper, *Leisure: The Basis of Culture* (New American Library, 1963), p. 69.

James Gaston: Faith, Reason and Christopher Dawson

1. *Modernity* usually refers to the period of time since the mid-seventeenth century that is characterized by what Pope Benedict XVI called "the dictatorship of relativism," a general rejection of tradition and hierarchy and a tendency to push religious ideas, influences and institutions to the margins of life. Modernity is also pluralistic—that is, it makes available a competing number of religions and philosophies or meta-narratives whose meanings are largely considered a matter for private, not public, concern.

2. "By *despair*, man ceases to hope for his personal salvation from God, for

help in attaining it or for the forgiveness of his sins. Despair is contrary to God's goodness, to his justice—for the Lord is faithful to his promises—and to his mercy" (*CCC*, 2091). Despair has also been used in twentieth-century French existentialist philosophy and literature to describe the revulsion and horror man feels when he realizes the universe is impersonal, random and purposeless.

3. Love Inn, then in Freeville, New York, was part of what sociologists have come to call the Jesus Movement, a Christian countercultural effort to reach young men and women who were alienated by more traditional forms of Christianity.

4. Phil Keaggy, for three years in a row, was voted one of the top finger-style guitarists by *Guitar Player* magazine readers. Phil won his first Dove award in 1988 for his instrumental album *The Wind and the Wheat*. Phil's second Dove Award came in 1992 for his Celtic-influenced *Beyond Nature*. Each year from 1998 to 2001, Phil has dominated the "Instrumental Record" category at the Doves, winning for *Invention*, *Acoustic Sketches*, *Majesty and Wonder* and most recently *Lights of Madrid*.

5. Christopher Dawson (1889–1970) entered the Catholic Church in 1914 and went on to be her leading cultural historian in the English-speaking world in the mid third of the twentieth century. Dawson held the Chauncey Stillman chair of Roman Catholic Studies at Harvard from 1958 to 1962. He believed that Christ was the center of human history. He taught that the history of the human race hinges on the unique divine event that gives spiritual unity to the whole historic process. History was intelligible. There was a grand narrative with meaning, direction, purpose. See his daughter's biography: Christina Scott, *A Historian and His World: A Life of Christopher Dawson* (New Brunswick, N.J.: Transaction, 1991).

6. Dawson's most influential book was *The Making of Europe: An Introduction to the History of European Unity* (1932). His Gifford Lectures were published as *Religion and the Rise of Western Culture* (1950), and lectures given while a professor at Harvard were published as *The Dividing of Christendom* (1967). The compilers of the European Union's charter have refused to acknowledge the Catholic roots of Europe in spite of appeals from the late Pope John Paul II and now Pope Benedict XVI. Both asked for specific mention of Europe's Christian roots in the preamble of the European

Union's new constitution. In an interview in *Le Figaro* magazine published in the summer of 2004, then-Cardinal Ratzinger deemed it a "mistake" to omit Europe's Christian roots in the European Union constitution, calling Europe a "cultural continent, not a geographical one" whose roots are Christian (cited in Michael J. Gaynor, "Pope Benedict Is Right: Europe Needs to Appreciate Its Christian Roots," www.catholic.org). See also George Weigel, *The Cube and the Cathedral: Europe, America and Politics Without God* (New York: Basic, 2006).

Father Pat Egan: Raised to New Life
1. Eucharistic Acclamation 4 from the Order of the Mass.

2. "It is in death...that pagan hopelessness finds its fullest manifestation. Pagan mourning vividly symbolizes this. Even in paganism, however, there is a sense that it ought not to be.... Violent mourning may thus yield to a quiet sorrow whose very quietness anticipates the blessed rest when sorrow is changed forever into the fullness of joy" (Gerhard Kittel and Gerhard Friedrich, *Theological Dictionary of the New Testament*, abridged in one volume, Geoffrey Bromiley, trans. [Grand Rapids: Eerdmans, 1985], p. 476). Compare Paul's attitude in 1 Thessalonians 4:13: "But we would not have you ignorant, brethren, concerning those who are asleep, that you may not grieve as others do who have no hope" (see verses 14–18; Hebrews 9:14–15).

3. François-Xavier Durrwell, *Christ Our Passover: The Indispensable Role of Resurrection in Our Salvation*, John F. Craghan, trans. (Liguori, Mo.: Liguori, 2004); also *The Resurrection* (New York: Sheed and Ward, 1960).

4. See *CCC*, 645, Matthew 28:17; Luke 24:30, 39–40, 41–43; John 20:20, 24–27; 21:9, 13–15.

5. Karl Marx (1818–1883), economist, is often named along with Darwin and Freud as one of the three most influential thinkers of the nineteenth century. He is probably best known for coauthoring, along with Friedrich Engels, the *Communist Manifesto* (1848), and he is called the father of dialectical materialism.

APPENDIX: A HISTORICAL SURVEY OF PERSONAL TESTIMONY IN THE SERVICE OF THE GOSPEL

1. See Richard Bauckham, *Jesus and the Eyewitnesses: The Gospels as Eyewitness Testimony* (Grand Rapids: Eerdmans, 2006)

2. See Ignatius of Antioch, Letter to the Romans 1:1; 4; Letter to the Philadelphians 6.

3. Justin Martyr, *II Apologia*, xviii, 1.

4. Tertullian, *Apologeticus*, chap. 50.

5. Augustine, *Confessions*, bk. 8, chaps. 6, 12.

6. The historical value of the *Liber Pontificalis* (editions printed in 537, 687, 891 and 1464) and *The Golden Legend* (*Legenda Aurea*, 1275) have been questioned in modern times with the advent of scientific historical methods. The critics are correct in their assessment that these two medieval books are not the kind of histories the modern reader expects, but that does not mean that these texts held no value for medieval people and hold no value for people of the twenty-first century. One translator of the *Liber Pontificalis*, Louise Ropes Loomis, called that text "a mesh of veritable fact, romantic legend, deliberate fabrication and heedless error" and yet praised it as a valid exposition of medieval culture and historical fact. See Louise Ropes Loomis, trans., *The Book of the Popes (Liber Pontificalis)* (New York: Octagon, 1965), p. x.

7. Many authors have attempted to explain Christian mysticism. A few good sources are Reginald Garrigou-Lagrange's two-volume *The Three Ages of the Interior Life*, Sr. M. Timothea Doyle, trans. (Rockford, Ill.: Tan, 1999); Ralph Martin's widely acclaimed recent success *The Fulfillment of All Desire: A Guidebook for the Journey to God Based on the Wisdom of the Saints* (Steubenville, Ohio: Emmaus Road, 2006); and finally a slim book by Iain Matthew, *The Impact of God: Soundings from St. John of the Cross* (London: Hodder and Stoughton, 1995), meant to sketch the thought of Saint John of the Cross but serving in addition to introduce some concepts and means of expression common to all Christian mystics.